The Social Context
of Pastoral Care

The Social Context of Pastoral Care

Defining the Life Situation

George M. Furniss

Westminster John Knox Press
Louisville, Kentucky

Scripture quotations from the New Revised Standard Version of the Bible are copyright © 1989 by the Division of Christian Education of the National Council of the Churches of Christ in the U.S.A. and are used by permission.

Book design by Drew Stevens
Cover design by Frank Perrone

First edition

Published by Westminster John Knox Press
Louisville, Kentucky

This book is printed on acid-free paper that meets the American National Standards Institute Z39.48 standard. ∞

PRINTED IN THE UNITED STATES OF AMERICA

94 95 96 97 98 99 00 01 02 03 — 10 9 8 7 6 5 4 3 2 1

Library of Congress Cataloging-in-Publication Data

Furniss, George M., date.
  The social context of pastoral care : defining the life situation
George M. Furniss. — 1st ed.
      p.   cm.
  Includes bibliographical references and index.
  ISBN 0-664-25436-5 (alk. paper)
  1. Pastoral counseling.   2. Sociology, Christian.   3. Church and
  social problems.   I. Title.
  BV4400.F87   1994
  253—dc20   94-8766

Contents

Preface

It is time someone said it (loudly): Sociology is "in the air" of pastoral care. Hints of sociology are evident on all sides: the feminist critique of traditional pastoral care, the concern for the "relational self," analyses of cross-cultural pastoral care, the introduction of liberation theology, and perhaps most striking, the popularity of family systems theory, nowhere more dramatized than in the use within clinical pastoral education and clergy practice of Edwin Friedman's book, *Generation to Generation*.

Sociologists point out that new ideas float around "in the air"— not coalescing as a distinct point of view—until structural mechanisms are put in place to codify and develop them. That pastoral care, and the theological enterprise more generally, has not seen sociological ideas reach a point of take-off is due in large part to the neglect of sociology in theological education (Schmidt 1978; Whitehead and Whitehead 1980, 173–74). Sociology, because it occupies an ill-defined position between Christian ethics and psychology, falls through the cracks of the seminary curriculum.

At later times in its history, a discipline often recovers elements of its early tradition that were left undeveloped, the roads not taken. Anton T. Boisen, a leading founder of the modern pastoral care movement, was a sociologist as well as a psychologist of religion (Pruyser 1967; Thornton 1970; Fowler 1990). The sociological thrust of Boisen's multifaceted mind was eclipsed by colleagues and followers who were oriented toward medicine, psychiatry, and psychology. Hence sociology has existed as a largely unheralded tributary of the pastoral tradition.

This book is both an ambitious and a modest project. On the one hand, it aims at introducing pastoral caregivers to an entire social scientific field, as complex, as ramified, and often as technical as contemporary sociology is. On the other hand, it seeks to do this in a suggestive rather than a comprehensive way, offering a "sampler" of sociological approaches that seem fruitful for pastoral caregivers. Later we will talk about the identity problem of pastoral caregivers in relation to their position in the middle between cultures. As I have written this book, I have been ever cognizant of being a person "in the middle": one foot in pastoral care, the other in sociology, with the limits that fact entails.

I have found it helpful to have in mind a particular group of readers as a concrete expression of the book's intended audience—the twenty-odd participants in a 1992 Eden Seminary pastoral care course, "Theological Diagnosis and Assessment." Professor Peggy Way invited me to share in the leadership of this class as a "sociological consultant." The students, a diverse mix of master of divinity and doctor of ministry candidates, chaplains, pastors, counselors, young and older, had backgrounds in theology and psychology but little sociology. As a result, the goal in presenting sociology to this class was to start with the basics and work from there. That approach orients this book.

Some argue that the day of general books on pastoral care is past; the specialized knowledge required to do pastoral care in specific areas of care (such as adult children of alcoholics, sexually abused women, hospital coronary care and oncology patients, and clients in pastoral psychotherapy) makes general books of limited use. I disagree with this point of view, for I believe that, whatever our specialty as pastoral caregivers, we need to preserve the sense of being Renaissance men and women, open to, and synthesizing alternative perspectives on our work. While most of the illustrations in this book come from hospital ministry and smaller church parish ministry—the fields of my experience—I believe that full-time pastoral counselors, specialists in other kinds of institutional ministry, and pastoral caregivers, both ordained and lay and in different congregational contexts, will find the general perspective set forth here of theoretical and practical use.

Some advance notice to the reader is needed about certain conventions of language used in this study. Following the usage of Larry Kent Graham (1992), the recipient of pastoral care is usually referred to as the "careseeker." This practice avoids problems arising from using terms associated with specific types of pastoral care: patient, client, parishioner, congregant, and counselee. The terms "modern society" and "modernity" are used throughout the book to refer to contemporary industrial and postindustrial societies. This usage is favored by most American sociologists. We hear the distinction made frequently in cultural analysis between modernism and postmodernism. The sociology of knowledge approach to modern culture informing this book is in certain, but not all, ways postmodernist in its thrust.

A glossary of sociological terms is provided at the end of the book, and these terms have been indexed as well. Also included is a section of biographical notes on the sociologists most prominently featured in the book.

Sociologists, because of their studies of power, language, and gender, were pioneers in the movement for the use of inclusive language. However, prior to the mid-seventies, sociologists were fond of using the generic term "men" or "man" for human beings. Today's author faces three options concerning quotations from these earlier writers: to omit all such quotes, to "clean up" the language to conform to present-day usage, or to pass on the texts as written. Each option is problematic, but I have chosen to use the last option, asking readers to make internal translation when noninclusive phrases appear.

Case material from my own pastoral work and that of others is presented here in a disguised form to eliminate any possibility of recognition. Personal details are altered in order to render the subjects unidentifiable, and at several points the cases are composites. It is with regret that details of cases are changed, for the sociological approach insists that the social context is integrally related to the individual's viewpoint and dynamics. The case of "Joyce" in chapter 3 is an undisguised case, and my special appreciation is extended to the subject for her permission to use her story.

I am indebted to many people for their contributions to this book, some through their broad influence in shaping my perspective, others through direct assistance with the book itself. At Pomona College, my interests in theology, philosophy, and sociology were stirred by Gordon Kaufman, Frederick Sontag, and Alvin Scaff, respectively. As a graduate student in sociology at Columbia University, I was especially influenced by Robert K. Merton, an inspired classroom lecturer, who opened for me wide vistas of social theory; by Ivan Vallier, who introduced me to the sociology of religion and was a good personal friend; and by

Immanuel Wallerstein, who understood global economic and political systems. As a very junior sociology instructor at Brooklyn College, I had occasional interaction with a faculty colleague, Peter L. Berger, whose influence became strong later through his writings when I moved toward theology. Making the transition from college teaching to seminary, ordination, and pastoral work, I found the support of Marvin Chaney and Roy Fairchild at San Francisco Theological Seminary invaluable, the former as a sociologically oriented biblical scholar and the latter as a pastoral counselor trained in social psychology.

The idea of this book came to me at a time when I worked as a staff chaplain at Sacred Heart General Hospital in Eugene, Oregon, and taught sociology as an adjunct faculty member at Northwest Christian College. I am indebted to these communities on either side of Alder Street. My chaplain colleagues in the hospital's Department of Pastoral Care have been my teachers, friends, and "sounding boards" for ideas: David Allison, Allen Duston, Mary Fleming, Walt Gray, Linda Harrell, Don Hefty, Jerry Heintzelman, Noel Hickie, Katherine McCarry, and Robert Scheri. David Allison read drafts of the manuscript and wins an award for being, in the most positive sense of the phrase, a "constructive critic." Another debt is to the directors of pastoral care and to clinical pastoral education supervisors in St. Louis and to a group of seminary pastoral care professors for the information they provided through interviews.

To William H. Swatos, Jr., a sociologist of religion, Episcopal Church vicar, and pastoral counselor, I owe a special debt for the concept of religious definitions of the situation. This concept is central to the sociological definition of pastoral care employed in this book. In an article, Swatos (1987) makes a convincing case for the use of this concept to orient a sociologically informed pastoral care. Swatos shares my understanding of pastoral caregivers as primarily religious counselors and not humanistic professionals.

Special appreciation goes to Don Browning, George Fitzgerald, Archie Smith, Jr., Peggy Way, and an anonymous reviewer of early draft chapters for their strong support of a book viewing pastoral care from the perspective of sociology. Thanks to Alexa Smith of Westminster John Knox Press, who began the editorial process, and to Harold L. Twiss, who skillfully completed it. Thanks also to our congregations, especially Westminster Presbyterian Church and

Peace Presbyterian Church in Eugene; to their pastors, Chuck Willming and John Huenink; and to our circle of friends in the Camps Farthest Out movement, a Christian renewal organization. My family has been much involved in this project. Our children, Kirsten, Astrid, Peter, and Ingrid—as well as their three spouses—took a strong interest in the book's emergence, and Peter and Ingrid gave their dad editorial and bibliographic help. I am indebted to my parents, George A. and Nell Furniss, for a "research grant" making it financially possible for me to take a "sabbatical" for writing. My wife Ruth, through her love, example, ideas, and patience, has made a major contribution. As a native of Denmark, Ruth, through her European viewpoint, makes every day of our life a cross-cultural experience. Ruth has strong lay pastoral care skills and her perspective, not radically feminist but unambiguously oriented to the situation of women, influences this book in many ways. As a professional reference librarian, Ruth has given me important computer bibliographic and interlibrary loan support.

This book asserts that sociology is a key resource for resolving the identity struggle confronting pastoral care today. The sociological perspective helps pastoral caregivers find their distinctive and proper "voice" in our modern secular age. To speak in family systems language, sociology contributes to the differentiation of the pastoral caregiver in the larger social system. The objective of this book is, quite simply, to show how.

G.M.F.

1. Sociology for Pastoral Care

Pastoral care displays the common tendency of disciplines to advance through a pattern of countervailing excess. Like a pendulum, the discipline's emphasis goes from one extreme to the other. The perspective of pastoral care, like all cultures and subcultures, has three types of orientation, one of which may be emphasized more than the others: cognitive orientations (What is reality? What is knowledge?), cathectic orientations (What feels good or bad?), and evaluative orientations (What is right? What is moral?). Nineteenth-century pastoral care majored in evaluative orientations, the moralistic exhortation much maligned in popular culture today. It minored in the cognitive sphere, the perpetuation of correct religious doctrine. Twentieth-century pastoral care, in reaction to these excesses and following the temper of the Freudian times, concentrated on the cathectic orientation, the heart over the head, working toward a new phenomenon sociologist Philip Rieff (1990) calls "the feeling intellect." The former emphases of pastoral care, the evaluative and the cognitive, were redefined as improper: moralism and judgmentalism on the one hand, rationalism and evangelism on the other.

Pastoral care's excessive preoccupation with emotion, feeling, and "heart" led to a countermovement. In *The Moral Context of Pastoral Care* (1976), Don Browning asks Karl Menninger's famous question: Whatever became of sin? His book argues for the resurrection of ethical guidance as a legitimate concern of pastoral care. The evaluative concern is echoed by feminists and ethnic minorities who demand that pastoral care grapple with social justice issues.

This book continues the countermovement to recover wholeness for pastoral care. Its focus is the cognitive orientation of pastoral care. How we feel (cathectic orientation) depends significantly on

1

our reality assumptions (cognitive orientations). What we decide is right and ethical (evaluative orientation) hinges also on our epistemology (the cognitive). Pastoral care has bought heavily into the cultural pluralism and cognitive relativism of modern culture; as caregivers, we see our role as supporting people along the road *they* have chosen, of being agenda-free, and of being client- (or person-) centered. Norms of tolerance and acceptance of others' viewpoints so dominate present-day pastoral care that caregivers are left confused and ambivalent about their identity as religious counselors and about the value of their theological tradition in the counseling process.

When unbalanced and malintegrated, cultural systems generate stress. Social psychologists call this stress "cognitive dissonance." Conflicting values make it impossible to steer a steady course and have a consistent identity. Lasting satisfaction of people's cathectic needs requires solution of both the evaluative and the cognitive problems. It feels good (cathexis) when we believe we are behaving responsibly (ethics). It also feels good when we believe that our life and actions are consistent with the basic nature of reality and the creation (cognitive orientation). In other words, the cognitive, cathectic, and evaluative dimensions are all tied up in one system and must be dealt with together.

The sociological approach to pastoral care is an invaluable resource for integrating the cognitive, cathectic, and evaluative orientations. Sociology demonstrates the constant circularity and dialectic of these orientations, the cognitive defining the cathectic, the evaluative reinforcing the cognitive, the cathectic energizing the cognitive. Throughout this book, we will watch how these feedback effects operate.

The Uniqueness of Pastoral Care

Pastoral care shares with psychoanalysis, humanistic psychology, and other forms of care and counseling—both individual and group—the focus on a therapeutic relationship of caregiver and careseeker. These therapeutic modalities also share an emphasis on attention to feelings, on active listening, and on the dynamics of transference and countertransference. Because of these common aspects, pastoral care has struggled to define its uniqueness. Differentiation of the pastoral caregiver's role has been complicated by the weight of negative tradition, the images of nineteenth-century "care of souls" to be avoided.

The sociological approach to pastoral identity emphasizes that caregiver and careseeker engage in dialogue within the social context of modernity. A crucial aspect of modernity is overwhelming pluralism, the situation where competing worldviews and perspectives—what sociologists call *definitions of the situation*—vie for recognition and hegemony. Pluralism creates the social psychological context for modern life, the shift from fate to choice. Premodern human existence was fraught with danger, violence, and physical uncertainty but a "symbolic universe" of established belief and social roles yielded cognitive stability. Modern existence eliminates those certainties; everything is up for grabs.

A sociological definition of pastoral care guides this entire study: *pastoral care is a dialogue exploring the possibility and implications of a religious definition of the careseeker's situation.* This definition of pastoral care combines three elements: the dialogic relationship shared by pastoral care with other therapeutic modalities, the careseeker's social psychological situation of awesome choice-making generated by modern pluralism, and the special role and competence of the pastoral caregiver as a religious counselor. The problems presented by the careseeker to the pastor, chaplain, or pastoral counselor are in many cases the same problems that this person would present to a psychologist or other counselor: loss, grief, guilt, meaninglessness, alienation, addiction, depression, sexuality, marriage, children, occupation, discrimination, injustice, violence, aging, and death, to name a few. The unique quality of pastoral care is the cognitive orientation that defines the character of the therapeutic exchange.

What specifically is meant by the terms of this sociological definition of pastoral care? *Dialogue* signifies two-way communication with relative equality of the conversational partners. Sociologists are sensitized to the power dimension of social interaction. There is a risk in all counseling situations for a hierarchical authority relationship to develop. Pastoral caregivers who are sensitive to this danger work to establish a more egalitarian relationship. Emphasizing the dialogical character of pastoral care gives recognition that both careseeker and caregiver are transformed by the pastoral encounter.

The verb *explore* indicates the tentative and always unfinished character of the pastoral care process. Careseeker and caregiver are engaged together in a joint activity of discovery. Exploration of new experiential territory, what each of us faces at successive stages of our life, generates some mixture of fright and adventure. Crucial in pastoral exploration is not only understanding the feelings a situation generates but also identifying the worldviews that govern our reaction to the situation.

Throughout this book, *religion* and *religious definitions of the situation* refer to beliefs, practices, and groupings oriented to transcendent or supernatural reality. Sociologists consider this a substantive definition of religion, since it relates to religion's object, God, the gods, or spiritual reality. This point needs to be made clearly, because another type of definition of religion—functional definition—is common today. The latter focuses on the individual's *attitude* toward cultural objects. People have an attitude of awe or reverence toward those objects they consider sacred in contrast to those objects they deem profane; a functional definition defines religion as whatever the individual recognizes as sacred. Atheism, nationalism, secular humanism, and rational materialism thus can be considered religious definitions of the situation using a functional definition but not when a substantive definition is employed. In other words, the sociological definition of pastoral care asks what are the possibilities and implications of *transcendent* worldviews for understanding the careseeker's situation.

To speak of the *possibility* of a religious definition of the situation recognizes the widespread doubt among modern people about spiritual or transcendent reality. The question is not whether some people today hold strong religious beliefs, for it is obvious to all that many in fact do. Rather the question is, can lucid, "with it," modern people who are responsibly engaged in the world choose religious definitions? Answering that question requires some understanding of the sociology of knowledge. The word *possibility* signifies difficulty but not impossibility as when sociologist Peter L. Berger (1979) subtitles a book, "Contemporary Possibilities of Religious Affirmation."

Religious definitions of situations, so long as they are not as totally idiosyncratic as the "Sheilaism" of one woman (Sheila by name) interviewed by Robert N. Bellah et al. (1985, 221), have a theological coherence and thereby exercise constraint. In our day of privatized and "personal" religion, this fact is often ignored.

Beliefs about God and the cosmic order have consequences for human social relationships. Thus the *implications* of a religious definition of the situation come to the fore. If A, then B follows. It is when exploring the implications of a religious definition of the situation that the prophetic and ethical character of religion impacts the pastoral care process.

Several comments on this definition of pastoral care are in order. First, by focusing on the communicative and dialogic aspect of pastoral care, this definition may give the misimpression that pastoral care is only happening when people are talking. The ministry of silence and presence has paramount significance in certain pastoral encounters. Moreover, pastoral discretion is obviously required when working with troubled persons regarding the careseeker's capacity for reflection. As a pastoral relationship develops, the opportunity increases for exploration of alternative definitions of the situation.

Second, as sociologist Anthony Giddens (1984) emphasizes, people's practical knowledge (what they *know* about relationships, society, and the world but *cannot* articulate in precise language) exceeds their discursive knowledge (what they *can* explain verbally). Much pastoral care happens at the practical knowledge level where we experience but cannot precisely articulate. Definitions of the situation are communicated nonverbally as well as verbally. Conflicting expressed and unexpressed definitions may be communicated simultaneously, the former verbally, the latter by nonverbal cues. The complexity of social encounters, where communication occurs on several levels at the same time, provides the fascinating subject matter of Erving Goffman, whose microsociological perspective we will examine later.

The sociological definition of pastoral care is given prominence at the outset to highlight this book's purpose. Put simply and directly, that purpose is to clarify and strengthen the identity of pastoral caregivers in contradistinction to the identities of other "helping professionals" whose numbers proliferate. In one sense, the book is an extended commentary on this sociological definition. Chapter 2, on the sociology of knowledge, focuses on the modern possibility of religious orientations. It also deals with the vital connection between religious belief-systems and religious communities, a connection attenuated in the social situation of modernity. Chapter 3, on careseekers' identity, examines the modern dilemma of identification—group and community commitment—versus differentiation—striving for individual autonomy—and how pastoral caregivers can help people resolve this conflict. The next two chapters deal with the implications of religious definitions of the situation. Chapter 4, on power, inequality, and empowerment, seeks to illuminate the complex power and social justice issues posed by and in pastoral encounters. Chapter 5, on the sociology of religion, distinguishes alienating and de-alienating religion, the former containing many extrinsic elements—"cultural trappings"—that contradict the original theological vision of the early religious movement. Here we examine how pastoral care deals with patriarchal, ethnocentric, and nonegalitarian religious perspectives. Chapter 6, on the institutional context of pastoral care, concerns the role conflicts of pastors, pastoral counselors, and especially institutional caregivers, analyzing the forces militating against clear pastoral identity and differentiation of the pastoral role. Chapter 7, analyzing pastoral care as a social process, presents a five-stage model of pastoral care and uses an extended case study to illustrate how the sociological perspective sheds light on the work of pastoral care.

A sociological understanding of pastoral care, emphasizing the religious definition of the situation, applies to all religious viewpoints, including not only Christianity but also such other faiths as Judaism, Islam, Buddhism, and Hinduism. The intended audience for this book is, however, Christian pastoral caregivers. The book stresses the religious formation of the effective Christian pastoral caregiver. He or she, as a religious counselor, cannot articulate in the pastoral dialogue the Christian religious option when the caregiver has little experience of that particular spiritual journey. Cultivating the encounter with God is the equivalent in pastoral care of the requirement in psychoanalysis for the analyst to undergo his or her own analysis.

The goal of pastoral care is, in short, assisting individuals and groups to find *adequate* definitions of their life situation. Unhealthy religion may contribute to persons' inadequate definitions of the situation. In our psychological age, the alternative to unhealthy religion has too often been thought to be no religion. However, the pastoral caregiver posits a second alternative, healthy religion, the adequate faith that J. B. Phillips so eloquently described in his classic little book, *Your God Is Too Small* (1953).

If the pastoral caregiver is to make a convincing case for healthy religion, this individual needs to manifest in his or her commitments and lifestyle that adequate faith.

What Is Sociology?

Much confusion exists in the general community over the boundaries of the different social sciences. Sociologists experience identity crises too! Thus, we need some clarity regarding the purview of sociology, anthropology, social work, and social psychology.

Gerhard and Jean Lenski give a useful definition of sociology in terms of what sociologists do.

> Sociology is the branch of modern science that specializes in the study of human societies. Its aims and interests are extremely broad. Some sociologists study the subunits that make up societies—such as communities, family groups, political parties, and churches. Others focus on societal processes—processes of urban growth, the political process, the educational process. Still others study various problems that afflict human societies—poverty, for example, or crime, or racial conflict. All these studies contribute to our understanding of the larger picture. (1974, 3)

Anthropologists could feel that this definition crowds in upon their territory, for they also study human societies. At one time an informal division of labor existed between sociologists and anthropologists, the former concentrating on modern societies, the latter researching traditional societies. The distinctive methodologies of the two fields corresponded to this division of labor, sociologists using survey methods and statistical analysis, whereas anthropologists employed participant-observation and field methods. Today some of this traditional division of labor continues to be observed, but the difference between sociology and anthropology has become very blurred; urban anthropologists are using sophisticated survey techniques, and sociologists who have always used qualitative as well as quantitative research methods use the former even more frequently. Sociology and anthropology are often united in joint academic departments, and the current rise of "departments of comparative sociology" signal that there is no real distinction between the subject matter of anthropology and sociology. When I speak in this book about sociology, a sociological perspective, and sociological theory, I mean the broad, combined perspective of both sociologists and anthropologists.

Social psychology studies the relationship between the individual and society and focuses on attitude-formation and the "social self." Although it is sometimes claimed by the psychologists, social psychology usually finds its academic home in sociology departments. Social psychologists have made a major contribution to contemporary social theory, an impact that will be continually recognized in this book.

Social work is an applied field of study that combines perspectives from several social sciences. Its intellectual mainstream lies more in psychology and psychotherapy than in sociology. For this reason, professional social work has much in common with present-day pastoral care. In institutional settings, this fact poses a major problem of role differentiation. For example, hospital staffs are often confused about the roles of medical social workers and chaplains. Physicians, nurses, and ward clerks lament: "How do we know who to call when you people seem to be doing the same thing?" This common situation underscores the problem of pastoral role-clarification that this book addresses.

The task of this book would be made easier if sociology and sociological theory possessed a unified and cohesive outlook. There is much ferment in sociology at this time. This is attributable to a distinctive problem of the social sciences that is not shared with the natural sciences: their findings affect the behavior of their subjects. The behavior of T-lymphocytes studied by a microbiologist doing AIDS research is not influenced by the journal article that scientist publishes. By contrast, a sociological report on the spread of AIDS among people generates changes in the behavior of the research subjects. Sociologists call this phenomenon institutional reflexivity; it causes value considerations to be much more prominent in social scientific research than in natural science. Attitudes toward the social order and social change, social "interests," invariably affect observations and the research process. Early sociologists like Max Weber (1947a) aspired to be "value-free," but in recent years most sociologists have become reconciled to the inevitable play of values in their researches and theory.

Consequently, sociological theory today, like the modern society it seeks to describe, is pluralistic. This fact complicates our task in explicating the value of the "sociological perspective" for pastoral care, for there is not one, but several perspectives. Randall Collins (1985) skillfully analyzes the apparent disarray of contemporary sociology, distinguishing three major sociological traditions. He designates these perspectives the Durkheimian tradition of Émile Durkheim, the Conflict tradition of Karl Marx, Friedrich Engels, and Max Weber, and the Microinteractionist tradition of the American pragmatists, especially George Herbert Mead, and of the European phenomenologists Edmund Husserl and Alfred Schutz. The Durkheimian tradition undergirded American academic sociology as expressed in the "orthodox consensus" of the structural-functionalism of Harvard's Talcott Parsons and Columbia's Robert K. Merton. The Conflict tradition came to the fore prominently in the 1970s as "radical sociology," developing the ideas of C. Wright Mills, Alvin Gouldner, and the Frankfurt School of critical sociology. The Microinteractionist tradition yielded symbolic interactionism, interpretive sociology, and ethnomethodology.

This book draws on all three of these sociological traditions. Ignoring any of these perspectives would truncate the analysis and deny us valuable resources. At several points, the different perspectives will be explicitly compared. Thus readers are challenged to multiperspectival points of view on two levels: first, the level of the three fields informing the perspective of pastoral care (theology, psychology, and sociology) and second, the level of multiple perspectives in sociology.

Theology and Sociology

Sociology is sometimes portrayed as the arch-enemy of theology.[1] The relativism of much sociology, its tendency to redefine all knowledge as socially situated ideology, and its attack on religious ideas as "collective representations" (projections) of the social order lead some to conclude that sociology and theology are incompatible and mutually antagonistic. An uneasy peace between the two disciplines has been maintained, however, by enforcing a division of labor. The province of sociology is thus said to be the empirical realm of observable phenomena, while that of theology is the nonempirical or metaphysical realm. Talcott Parsons was a primary enforcer of this division of labor, arguing strongly that sociologists had little business making critical remarks about the truth-claims of theologians.

Those sociologists who adhere to a "hard relativist" position, maintaining that all knowledge is absolutely relative, stand on shaky philosophical ground. Their intellectual stance contravenes logic, for the superior wisdom of the knower who makes such an assertion must be equally relative. One of my sociology students in an exam articulated the logical contradiction of the "hard relativist" position in the following amusingly awkward but essentially correct sentence: "This statement is not logical to say that the truth is that there is no truth does not make sense." As Peter Berger (1969) points out, the sociology of knowledge "relativizes the relativizers." Berger's more intellectually defensible sociological position, what we could call "soft relativism," assumes the existence of absolute truth but asserts that each person's knowledge of that truth is conditioned by social location and personal experience.

Contrary to what one might think on first acquaintance with sociologists, who are not striking for their religiosity, sociology itself can be understood as a major support of the theological enterprise. While the positivist tradition of sociology through Durkheim exerts a secularizing influence, the phenomenological tradition through Alfred Schutz and Peter Berger clearly recognizes the legitimacy of different modes of consciousness, among them the religious. In contrast to the psychology undergirding much current pastoral care, which is strongly rationalistic and antithetical to religious consciousness, the phenomenological tradition of sociology is open to religion. *Unlike most contemporary psychology, present-day sociology, because it acknowledges the validity of different modes of consciousness, is a vital cognitive mooring for religious thought today.*

There is common ground between sociology, contemporary theology, and pastoral care in their attraction to process thought. Talcott Parsons, a major social systems theorist, was significantly influenced by Alfred North Whitehead, the progenitor of process philosophy. Process theology, through Charles Hartshorne, Bernard Loomer, and John B. Cobb, Jr., is also rooted in Whiteheadian philosophy. Process theology, because of its perceived congeniality with modern ecological and social systems thinking, appeals to a number of theoreticians of pastoral care, including Gordon Jackson (1981) and Larry Kent Graham (1992).

Although there exists an affinity between sociology and process theology, this book's sociological approach to pastoral care should not be thought to disparage traditional trinitarian Christian theology. One of the most sociologically oriented theologies in recent decades, Joseph Haroutunian's *God with Us: A Theology of Transpersonal Life* (1965), is solidly based in traditional trinitarianism. Trinitarian theology is, in fact, undergoing a remarkable renascence in Catholic (LaCugna 1992) and Protestant (Peters 1993) circles. This theological project restores the original intent of trinitarian doctrine, an understanding of God's salvific relationship to the world, and seeks to banish the concern that caused trinitarian theology to come into disrepute in the modern era, the medieval obsession with the inner workings of the Trinity.

Trinitarian theology, especially in its new (that is, old) expression, deals richly and profoundly with the divine-human encounter. Some accretions upon the early theology that developed historically we must repudiate, especially its improper justification of patriarchal and hierarchical social structures. That said, I want to state at the outset so the reader will understand my theological stance, that as a pastor and chaplain, doing pastoral care daily with troubled people, traditional Christian theology—not natural theology or process theology—has been my greatest resource. For me, knowledge of sociology with its emphasis on self-in-relationship reinforces my appreciation of the basic trinitarian Christian message.

How Sociology Is "in the Air" of Current Pastoral Care

Now that a sociological definition of pastoral care has been introduced and sociology has been defined, the link can be established between this book and the critiques of current pastoral care. These critiques are what lead me to the conclusion that sociology is "in the air" of pastoral theology and care. A new paradigm of pastoral care that unites psychology, theology, and sociology is emerging. If we do a content analysis of the recent critiques of pastoral care, we can discern five different "camps" of critics. To be sure, there is overlapping among some critics who combine two or more thrusts. The common thread of these otherwise different critiques is the sociological theme.

As was noted earlier, one group of critics of the status quo is the religious ethicists. Don S. Browning is the leader of this camp. In *The Moral Context of Pastoral Care*, he asserted:

> On the whole, recent theory and practice of pastoral care have been without an ecclesiology, without an interpretation of modern cultural and institutional life, and without a social ethic. (1976, 21)

Then in a later book, Browning (1983) speaks of the estrangement of care from ethics and the movement in pastoral care toward ethical neutrality. Still later, he (1987) provides a comprehensive critique of the major modes of psychotherapy from the point of view of religious and philosophical ethics. Browning asserts that unquestioned sociological assumptions[2] reside implicitly in the humanistic psychologies of Carl Rogers, Abraham Maslow, and Fritz Perls, assumptions that pastoral counselors have imported into pastoral care along with these popular therapeutic modalities. Other critics in this group are Stephen Pattison (1988) in England, and as we will see below, Archie Smith, Jr. (1982).

The second kind of criticism of existing pastoral care comes from the systems theorists. E. Mansell Pattison in his article, "Systems Pastoral Care" (1972) and his book, *Pastor and Parish: A Systems Approach* (1977) made some of the earliest statements of this perspective. The thrust of Pattison's approach, which he draws from social psychiatry, is now being incorporated in much pastoral care influenced by family systems theory. Under the impact of the latter perspective, the focus on individual clients or patients is held to be too narrow; rather the entire family is understood as the locus of care. Instinctively, when doing pastoral counseling with an individual careseeker, we now append to the statements of that individual the following qualifier: "This is the way this particular person in the system perceives the problem." The systems theory approach has alerted pastoral caregivers to the values of counseling families as units.

Pattison understands church congregations as social systems. The systemic perspective sees the local parish church as a living organism with functional subsystems. Organizational health or sickness of the congregation depends upon the degree to which critical functions are being performed. Pattison views the identity of the church pastor in systemic terms:

> I see the pastor as essentially a shepherd of systems. The pastor functions to nurture and guide the subsystems of the church. The pastoral role is determined by the pastor's systemic identity. For pastors, doing and being go together. And pastoral care is care of the *church* as a living system. (1977, 50)

Although couched in such perhaps unfamiliar terms of systems theory as holism, open synergy, and isomorphism, Pattison's approach to pastoral care as "systems pastoral care" is very comprehensible and represents a real paradigmatic breakthrough.

Using a different systems approach, William H. Swatos, Jr., sets forth a critique of pastoral psychology in his provocative article, "Clinical Pastoral Sociology." Summarizing this approach, the author says:

> In particular, the situational approach frees clinical pastoral sociology from the medical model inasmuch as the possibility for a "real" religious definition of a situation grants institutional independence to religion and its practitioners. (1987, 158)

Swatos stresses the need for a theoretical base for pastoral care that markedly differentiates the minister as a religious professional doing pastoral care from the minister who poses as a humanistic professional. Larry Kent Graham's recent book, *Care of Persons, Care of Worlds* (1992), a systems approach to pastoral care, belongs in this second group of critiques.

The third camp of critics stands within the tradition of mainstream pastoral care but calls for redefinition of the pastoral care task. Charles Gerkin (1984, 1986), Donald Capps (1984), and James Fowler (1987) are representative of this camp. This critique stresses the pluralistic character of the modern society, the pastoral care provider as the representative of the Christian community, and the importance of biblical narrative as the structure of meaning for fragmented and disoriented modern people. The forerunner of this critique was H. Richard Niebuhr whose book, *The Responsible Self* (1963), combines sociological and theological analysis. Gerkin's title, *Widening the Horizons: Pastoral Responses to a Fragmented Society (1986)*, sums up in brief the thrust of this critique. Fowler stresses pastoral care as the process of guiding Christians in their search for Christian vocation. Stanley Hauerwas (1981), a Christian ethicist, bridges this and the ethicist camps. These critics might collectively be called the *hermeneutic revisionists*.

Criticism of pastoral care comes from a fourth "camp," liberation theology. Of course, a large literature centered on the seminal works of Gustavo Gutiérrez, Paulo Freire, Juan Luís Segundo, and José Míguez Bonino sets forth this theological position. In pastoral care, Harvey Seifert and Howard Clinebell (1974) represent an early version of this perspective, and Clinebell in a later book (1981) gives it further articulation. Charlotte Holt Clinebell in her book, *Counseling for Liberation* (1976), voices this critique of pastoral care with special emphasis on gender liberation. Archie Smith, Jr., although he touches on all the critical camps, belongs primarily here. His important book, *The Relational Self: Ethics and Therapy from a Black Church Perspective* (1982), is written from the liberation theology point of view of the African-American church but incorporates the critique of the religious ethicists and the critique of the systems theorists. Rubem Alves (1977), Rebecca Chopp (1987), Rebecca Chopp and Duane Parker (1990), Homer Bain (1986), and Robert Kinast (1980) can be included in this camp of critics as well as Gail Unterberger (1990) and the feminist pastoral caregivers whose articles appear in Maxine Glaz and Jeanne Moessner (1991).

Liberation theology directs attention to the oppressive social structures that limit human development and to the coming reign of God, which overcomes these unjust and stifling structures. This critique of pastoral care is reminiscent of the New Left critique of psychology articulated in the 1960s, a critique that carried the name "radical therapy." Those associated with this thrust in psychology objected to the unpolitical character of psychoanalysis and much psychotherapy, saw the traditional psychotherapeutic relationship as largely sexist and racist, and demanded that the goal of therapy not be adjusting the client to the stultifying structures of modern technocratic capitalism but rather empowering the individual to engage in purposive action to change the unjust system. Pastoral care conducted from the feminist and radical ethnic minority points of view often combines the perspectives of radical psychology and liberation theology.

The fifth and last group of critics speak about pastoral care from "outside the camp." These are nontheologians concerned about broad social trends who judge the various psychotherapies, because of their individualistic ethos, to be destructive of the social fabric. Sociologist Robert N. Bellah and his associates in their well-known book, *Habits of the Heart* (1985), engage in indirect criticism of pastoral care. This book analyzes the therapeutic mentality of modern America. The research involved the intensive interviewing of subgroups of middle-class white Americans, among which was a sample of Protestant ministers and seminarians engaged in psychotherapeutic approaches to clinical pastoral education. This camp of critics draws its point of view from the larger critique of the psychologically oriented society identified with such sociologists as David Riesman (1950), Philip Rieff (1966), Philip Slater (1970), and such other cultural critics as Christopher Lasch (1978).

These five critical camps—the religious ethicists, the systems theorists, the hermeneutic revisionists, the liberation theologians, and the antipsychology culture critics—include a broad spectrum of religious and political positions. Religious liberals and conservatives populate the different groups, and political conservatives, liberals, and radicals are found among these critics. The common thread of these critiques is, in fact, the sociological thrust. The critics insist that the social context—relational, moral, and societal—of pastoral care must receive greater attention. The locus of pastoral care shifts from the troubled individual to the individual-society nexus. From client-centered therapy, we move to triadic pastoral care with the three points of the triangle being God, the self, and the society. These points correspond to the three disciplines informing pastoral care: theology, psychology, and sociology.

We turn now to the sociology of knowledge that sets forth the reality assumptions—the cognitive orientation—characteristic of modernity. This is the epistemological context for both pastoral caregiver and careseeker and, as such, dramatically affects the pastoral care process.

2. The Sociology of Knowledge and Pastoral Care

Pastoral care today happens in a highly pluralistic social context. Competing beliefs—secular versus religious, traditional female versus career woman, "macho" man versus "new" man, old industry versus global environment—whirl about. Established patterns give way to confusing changes. Careseekers confront choices on all sides: lifestyles, relationships, family patterns, careers, politics, religion. Berger, Berger, and Kellner (1973) aptly characterize the rootless cognitive world of modern people as the "homeless mind."

This chapter focuses on the possibility today of careseekers choosing religious perspectives to understand their lives and problems. Religion in the modern society leads a precarious and unstable existence. Through the sociology of knowledge, we will examine the difficulties our careseekers experience "thinking religiously."

The sociology of knowledge approach gives the pastoral caregiver an unaccustomed vantage point for understanding the careseeker.[1] Much of present-day pastoral care involves helping people resolve intrapsychic conflict and find personal integration. Components of the counseled person's mental world do not fit. Guilt, anger, anxiety, addiction, distrust, and confusion result. As caregivers, we seek to understand the conflicts from *inside* the careseeker's cognitive world. Our careful listening, questioning, and paraphrasing help us—to the greatest extent possible—"see" how life looks and feels from the other's perspective. The nonjudgmental and agenda-free stance to which we aspire contributes to the achievement of this objective of "taking the role of the other."

The sociology of knowledge adds another dimension to our pastoral understanding of the counseled person. It looks at the individual's cognitive world from the *outside*, asking what are its reality assumptions and what social mechanisms support that particular mode of consciousness. The "givens" of modern everyday "taken-for-granted" knowledge—the definitions of cognitive truth, aesthetic beauty, and social morality—are understood not as fixed or immutable but as *options* among alternative worldviews. People rarely perceive their core definitions of reality as a choice. It is for this reason that the sociology of knowledge is a liberating force enhancing human freedom.

The sociology of knowledge deals primarily with the "taken-for-granted" world of everyday life. Knowledge here is not advanced knowledge or scientific knowledge or cultural elite knowledge (these are dealt with in the sociology of science and the sociology of the arts); rather it is the common knowledge—the shared understandings—of the adult population of a society. The basic assumptions of everyday life—interpersonal exchanges, motives, values, unquestioned routines—are the subject matter of the sociology of knowledge. What the "natural man or woman" (which is all of us most of the time) does automatically, the sociologist questions. What is taken for granted in normal social life, the sociology of knowledge does not take for granted. This capacity to make our everyday social life the object of investigation is what C. Wright Mills (1967) called "the sociological imagination." Its goal is "thinking ourselves away" from the familiar routines of daily life in order to look at them anew.

This present chapter builds up the perspective of the sociology of knowledge by introducing a series of sociological concepts: culture, definition of the situation, the social construction of reality, modes of consciousness, pluralization of life-worlds, structural differentiation, and secularization. Each of these concepts has particular usefulness for pastoral caregivers struggling to achieve more differentiated pastoral identity and to work effectively in the modern pluralistic situation.

Culture

As pastoral caregivers, we are most aware of culture when we deal with a cross-cultural situation.[2] Early in my hospital ministry, I was working with a young man who was battling a critical lung disease. When he died, his wife, who was Thai, manifested a grief reaction totally foreign to me. Alternately, she wept quietly, then she prostrated herself across his body, shaking him and shouting for him to wake up. Although I had read about extremely emotive grief reactions in the literature on non-Western cultures, this was the first time I actually witnessed such an expression. The Thai woman's alternating quiet and almost violent behavior continued for almost an hour. Fortunately, little active pastoral care seemed expected or needed, and I was "present" more as an observer of a strange and unpredictable cultural phenomenon. Nearly every pastoral caregiver experiences situations like this where his or her cultural assumptions are inoperative.

Few human reactions involve a direct response to a stimulus. To be sure, there are autonomic responses to painful stimuli such as withdrawing one's hand from a hot surface. Most human action, however, involves an intermediate step between stimulus and response: *interpretation*. This step often takes only a split second and consists of identifying or classifying the stimulus. As Walter Lippmann said, "First we look, then we name, and only then do we see."[3] Interpretation happens even in such "automatic" patterns as seeing a red traffic light and putting on the car brakes. Mentally, we ask what the red light means in that particular situation: Did it just change? (and therefore I have a chance to get through), Is it three A.M.? (and therefore enforcement of the traffic laws unlikely), Is the light functioning or is it "stuck"? Whatever the stimulus, except in the infrequent autonomic situations, our response is governed by the outcome of the interpretation process.

The symbolic apparatus involved in people's interpretation is what sociologists and anthropologists call their culture. Culture is the symbols and their meanings that human beings carry as mental baggage wherever they go. The culture represents the set of cognitions, cathexes, and evaluations that constitute the particular society's worldview. It gives the individual guidance about how to think, how to feel, and how to act. That we do not directly experience the world but that our reactions are mediated by culture is signified by the idea that we live in a "symbolic universe."

If our responses to the myriad stimuli bombarding us from the physical and social world were unmediated by our culture, we would experience such sensory overload as not to be able to survive. Our culture organizes our perceptions in ways that make our world meaningful and habitable. Of the total number of possible stimuli to which we might react, our culture defines that smaller and more manageable number of stimuli that are important and warrant attention. Hence social life involves selective perception. Our culture operates like Polaroid sunglasses filtering out "extraneous" stimuli and focusing our attention on "relevant" stimuli. Comparison of the development of language between different societies illustrates how selective perception works. For example, the Nuer people, a nomadic African tribe, have several hundred words in their language for cattle and cattle-raising, thus indicating the importance of accurate perceptions of subtle sensory differences concerning their herds for maintaining their way of life (Evans-Pritchard 1940).

Definitions of the Situation

The intervening stage of interpretation between stimulus and response constitutes the *definition of the situation*. W. I. Thomas, the sociologist to whom we owe this concept, states:

> Preliminary to any self-determined act of behavior there is always a stage of examination and deliberation which we may call *the definition of the situation*. (1923, 42)

The visitor to our home, confronting our jumping, barking golden retriever dog, must resolve the definitional issue before responding to her: Is this an excited, friendly, gentle dog, or is this a suspicious, angry, potentially harmful dog? Tangie is the former, but it takes a few moments for people to figure this out.

Another way of defining a society's culture, besides saying that it is symbols and their meanings, is to assert that it is the complex mental guidebook people utilize to formulate the myriad definitions of the situation forced on them every day.

A brief hospital encounter illustrates how we form definitions of the situation. A couple standing in the hospital elevator watched me press my destination floor button and noticed the staff badge that identified me as a chaplain. The man remarked, "We're sure glad you're not going to the same floor as we are."

My quizzical look must have expressed my lack of understanding, because he quickly added, "Oh, my father is on the fifth floor. We'd worry he was in trouble if you were going there."

I smiled. "We see lots of people who aren't having bad trouble," I replied.

The man in a split second combined three pieces of knowledge: his awareness of his ill father's hospital location, his perception of chaplains as the "death-and-dying" people, and his observation of my destination. In that moment, his emotions went from neutral to worry to relief. By combining a series of selective perceptions, we form a definition of the situation.

Stating concisely the social implication of definitions of the situation, W. I. Thomas and his wife, Dorothy Swaine Thomas, formulated probably the most famous sentence in all sociology, widely known as the Thomas Theorem: *If men define situations as real, they are real in their consequences* (1928, 572). In other words, the subjective "definition of the situation" is just as important as the objective situation in its social effects.

Self-fulfilling prophecies (Merton 1957, 421–36) illustrate the Thomas Theorem: a false definition of the situation evokes new behavior, which then makes the originally false conception come true. For example, a child may be (incorrectly) labelled as a "slow learner"; teachers act on the basis of this "information" by placing the child in custodial type classes. The false prophecy then becomes true: the child manifests obvious learning disabilities. Entire social groups—racial, ethnic, and gender "minorities"—fall subject to self-fulfilling prophecies; a false definition of reality (intelligence, aptitudes, capacities) becomes so widely institutionalized in the society that situations that might provide evidence to disprove it never arise. In short, culture—the complex of a society's definitions of reality—is the filter through which the individual's perceptions of the physical and social world pass, and that individual's actions are responses, not to the objective reality, but to the cultural definition.

How providing an alternative definition of the situation affects people's reaction is demonstrated by a memorial service conducted by a hospital chaplain. Tom, a popular hospital orderly, had committed suicide. His frequent bouts of depression were known to the chaplains who had counseled him, but not to the general hospital staff, who saw Tom only as a good-spirited fellow employee. The chaplains met with groups of employees grieving Tom's death, where concern about his salvation surfaced among religiously oriented staff. The chaplain who led the memorial service included in his message the following story: A pastor was counseling a woman whose husband had committed suicide. The woman was extremely distressed that her husband's salvation was cancelled by his act of self-destruction. The pastor asked the woman, "If John had died of a heart attack, would you have any question of his salvation?" The woman replied, "Oh, of course not!" The pastor then asserted, "John died of a mind attack. Do you think God would treat him that much differently?" The wife said, "No. I see what you mean. That really helps me think about this." Many people who attended this service, which was held in the hospital's auditorium, remarked how this change of the definition of the situation caused them to feel better about Tom's death.

The Social Construction of Reality

Berger and Luckmann (1966) sum up the perspective of the sociology of knowledge in their conception of the social construction of reality.[4] This perspective defines the relationship between the individual and the society in terms of three generalizations about the social world that they call "dialectical moments."

Society is a human product. This "moment" is what the authors call *externalization*. "Men together produce a human environment, with the totality of its socio-cultural and psychological formations" (1966, 51). Human biology provides only the outer limits for social life. The specific social patterns, although their historic origins may not be well understood, reflect the creativity and diversity of human invention. For members of a traditional society remote from culture contact, this dialectical moment is obscured, since social change might happen at such a glacial pace that no one can perceive it. The social order as part of the cosmic order is understood as created by the gods. Its human production is invisible.

Society is an objective reality. This is the dialectical moment of *objectification*. Social norms and institutions, while human products, are experienced by people as having a facticity independent of their human creation. French sociologist Émile Durkheim (1938) stressed the idea that social facts exert an objective power that belies their origin in human subjectivity. A primary example of objectification is language. The assignment of meaning to particular sounds or markings is a social process reflecting quite arbitrary decisions by people. However, as a totality, a society's language looms as an objective reality that the individual feels little power to affect or change.

The human being is a social product. This third moment describes the transmission of the social world to the next generation and its shaping influence, through the process of *internalization.* The socialization process involving internalization or identification results in the individual learning to define "truth," "beauty," and "morality" in the culturally prescribed ways. The maturing person thereby develops a social conscience and becomes self-policing, prejudging alternative courses of action in terms of the now introjected prevailing norms.

Modes of Consciousness

Sociological phenomenologists point out that human beings distinguish multiple levels of reality. Alfred Schutz (1962), bringing the thought of Husserl into sociology, speaks of four human modes of consciousness.[5] The mode of "everyday life" is the wide-awake sense of normal daily routine in work and family. The "religious" mode of consciousness involves a sense of awe and mystery, experienced in the dream-state and under conditions of devotional or ceremonial concentration. A "scientific" mode of consciousness exists when people adopt a systematic attitude of doubt and invoke careful rules for establishing the truthfulness of reality-statements. The "aesthetic" mode of consciousness emphasizes the appearance rather than the substance of things and finds enjoyment in sensory illusions.

The phenomenological tradition of the sociology of knowledge locates its basic perspective in this multidimensional view of human consciousness. The term, *phenomenology,* coming from Edmund Husserl, means a study of human consciousness open to the full complexity of the subjective experience of the observed human subject, the "phenomenon." This is not an approach that imposes the observer's theoretical straitjacket, the modern "scientific" tendency that Husserl called reductionistic. Here reductionism means the improper habit of looking at a multidimensional phenomenon in a unidimensional way. This tradition of the sociology of knowledge understands selective perception as cognitive reductionism, whereby the individual's complex consciousness with its sense of multiple levels of reality is often viewed in an oversimplified ("scientific") way, thus "reducing" its complexity.[6] The sociology of knowledge generates a critique of modern culture. Modern Western culture—secularistic, capitalistic, individualistic, and rationalistic—is understood by sociologists of knowledge as no exception to the rule that cultures are socially constructed symbolic universes encompassing myriad selective perceptions about reality. Failure to grasp this cardinal truth causes the cultural myopia of "modernism." This excessively narrow viewpoint is based on the belief that modern society has progressed or advanced to such a position of superior knowledge as to be immune to the heretofore endemic selective perception involved in culture. The "scientific" mentality, enshrining empirical methodology and logical positivist rationality, becomes defined as an unassailable standard, what sociologist Robert Bellah (1989) calls a "metalanguage," to judge all perspectives.

This judgment of the assumed superiority of modern culture is well stated by Peter Berger:

> Modern consciousness is one of many historically available forms of consciousness. . . . It is possible that modern consciousness, while expanding man's awareness of some aspects of the universe, has made him lose sight of other aspects that are equally real. (1979, 8–10)

Our modern theory of knowledge, as enshrined in the "metalanguage" noted earlier, emphasizes scientifically demonstrable "facts" and causes modern people to lose sight of other kinds of knowledge, especially religious, moral, and intuitive knowledge.

Sociologists signal their critical attitude toward this reigning theory of knowledge when they call it "scientism," a term used by Husserl and by more contemporary thinkers to designate the modern cultural myopia. Scientism, as used here, refers to a worldview rooted in the outmoded perspective of nineteenth century science, a perspective long discarded by today's advanced theoretical scientists, which makes sharp distinctions between "fact" and "fiction." Sociologist Robert Bellah asserts that science has its legitimate place but must be prevented from encroaching on other territories of knowledge. In his words, "Science turns out to be just one more 'tribal tradition,' or set of tribal traditions,

whose validity must be tested in the general discussion and practice of human beings" (1989, 78). Careful analysis of the multiple
levels of meaning, the domains of knowledge, is required as the
corrective to such cultural hegemony.

Berger holds that modern people have a *choice* about their
mode of consciousness. His attitude comes through strongly in his
reaction to the theology of Rudolf Bultmann. In his famous article
of the early 1940s, "New Testament and Mythology," Bultmann
described the mythological New Testament worldview as depicting a three-story universe: Earth exists in the middle where beings
from "up above" and "down below" do cosmic battle. Bultmann
held that modern people are *incapable* of accepting or grasping the
mythological view of the universe. He wrote:

> One cannot [*man kann nicht*] use electric light and radio, call
> upon modern medicine in case of illness, and at the same time
> believe in the world of spirits and miracles of the New Testa-
> ment. (Quoted in Berger 1979, 105)

Berger rejects the uncategorical character of Bultmann's assertion.
Berger's theory of modern pluralism shows the reasons why modern people have *more difficulty* grasping the New Testament
worldview, but Berger says a bold "nonsense" to Bultmann's assertion that modern people *cannot* understand or accept the biblical worldview.

> All [translation models like Bultmann's] share the conviction
> that modern man stands on some sort of cognitive pinnacle,
> from which he can survey and overcome the shortcomings of all
> his predecessors. (1979, 119)

Berger raises the constant question whether modern people have
not lost critically valid religious insights such as the whole idea of
transcendence.

Pluralization of Life Worlds

Urban life, global communication, and massive culture contact
contribute to the pluralization of modern peoples' life-worlds.
Gabriel LeBras, a French sociologist of religion, studied how devout
Catholic men and women from Brittany, a predominantly rural
province renowned for its people's religiosity, suddenly became ag-
nostics when they migrated to urban Paris. LeBras even speculated

(not seriously) that there was a spot in the Gare du Nord, the Paris railway station where the Bretons disembarked, that had some magical power to rob the urban immigrants of their faith.

As Berger, Berger, and Kellner observe, the pluralization of modern societies means that what was a matter of fate in the traditional society—occupation, marriage arrangements, religion— becomes, in the modern era, a matter of choice. They assert that religious uncertainty is a key aspect of the modern "homeless mind."

> Social-psychologically, the same forces of pluralization have undermined the taken-for-granted status of religious meanings in individual consciousness. In the absence of consistent and general social confirmation, religious definitions of reality have lost their quality of certainty and, instead, have become matters of choice. Faith is no longer socially given, but must be individually achieved—be it by a wrenching act of decision along the lines of Pascal's "wager" or Kierkegaard's "leap"—or more trivially acquired as a "religious preference." Faith, in other words, is much harder to come by in the pluralistic situation. The individual now becomes conversion-prone, as it were. Just as his identity is liable to fundamental transformations in the course of his career through society, so is his relation to the ultimate definitions of reality. (1973, 81)

That pluralism weakens religious certainty, that having conflicting voices all around makes people feel less secure about their religious perspective than if they received steady confirmation of their worldview, is often evidenced in hospital ministry. An AIDS patient in his late twenties told me that his religious faith seemed of little help in dealing with the crisis of his illness and impending death. He was raised in a churchgoing family, was active in the high school youth program, and maintained some church connection through college. His present circle of friends, however, was made up of persons representing diverse religions and no religion. His roommate was what he termed a "hard-core" Buddhist who engaged in daily religious rituals. Among other things, this young man told me that he questioned a Christian theology that pronounced judgment on devout non-Christians like his good friend. It was clear the total pluralism of this careseeker's social world caused him to find little comfort in the assurances of the religion of his childhood and youth.

Another conversation focuses precisely the problem of pluralism and religious choice. A young male hospital patient and I were talking about religious faith. The young man said he desperately wanted to "believe." However, listening to the multitude of religious voices, he heard "truth" being defined in radically different ways by the various faith-communities, all claiming divine authority. His question of me was, "Chaplain, how does one know?" This man's question sharply highlights the problem of religious authority in a pluralistic age. Pastoral caregivers challenge careseekers to make the leap of faith, but given the pluralism of the social environment, the careseeker asks the very legitimate question, Where should I leap? This is the dilemma that gives rise to what Berger calls "the heretical imperative." Since there is no longer a generally recognized standard of religious orthodoxy, all persons construct their own worldviews. Worldviews are not received and passed on in relatively unchanged form as in premodern times. The modern individual must *assemble* a worldview, much like children putting together Lego sets. Berger, Berger, and Kellner call this *briccolage*, the French word for "do-it-yourself" construction projects.

Structural Differentiation

The sociology of knowledge approach to the problem of modern religious consciousness directs attention to structural characteristics of the modern society. Understanding this larger structural context is crucial for grasping the social psychological experience of our careseekers, their "homeless minds." Pastoral care authors such as Gerkin (1986) often touch on the psychodynamic consequence without explicating the social structural causes.

Two kinds of pluralism are present in modern societies. On the one hand, there is the pluralism caused by culture contact, where persons having different religious and value perspectives closely interact, in cities for example. On the other hand, there is the pluralism caused by institutional autonomy, where the sectors of the society—each having its own distinctive values—pull apart, thus leaving the society without a central integrating value system. Pluralism of this second kind, a key to secularization, requires our attention at this point.

The fragmentation of values and worldview caused by institutional autonomy results from the historic process of *structural differentiation.* Sociologists use this term to describe the process whereby one multifunctional system divides into two or more systems each with a specific function. A preliminary way to conceive of structural differentiation is to think of the development of a more complex social division of labor. A society with a simple division of labor having only a small number of social positions, for example, hunters (virtually all adult males) and gatherers (most adult women), becomes more complex as new positions evolve. This preliminary conception must be considerably developed in order for us to grasp how sociologists understand structural differentiation and its social psychological impact. To attain this more comprehensive conception, we must review some very basic elements of the sociological perspective. Here we deal with key insights of the functionalist tradition in sociology, the dominant viewpoint in American academic sociology through the mid-1960s.

First, we will look at social functions, then at social systems. *Social functions* are positive consequences for social life of particular social behaviors. Negative consequences of social behaviors are termed *dysfunctions.* Sociologists focus their attention principally on the social rules or *norms* that govern people's behavior, asking whether those norms generate functional or dysfunctional behaviors. When sociologists speak of *social structures*, they are referring to complexes of social rules (norms) that govern particular spheres of a society's life. Functional analyses by sociologists investigate what are the specific functions (and dysfunctions) of particular social structures. For example, incest taboos, virtually universal among human societies yet varying in the specific rules prohibiting sexual relations between immediate kin, are structures that have been subjected to functional analysis. A genetic rationale for such taboos, based on the biological consequences of inbreeding, depends on scientific knowledge not available to traditional peoples. Rather, sociologists and anthropologists understand the function of incest taboos to be fostering social integration and the authority of the parental generation. By prohibiting persons from having sexual relations with or marrying members of the immediate family or, in some societies, clan, social bonds through marriage are created with other families and clans. By banning such relations between parent and child, the united authority of the parents vis-à-vis the children is established.

Parsons (1977) identifies four broad social functions for which every society must make adequate provision in order to survive and maintain stability. He terms these functions functional imperatives. The first imperative is *economic*, the adaptation of the society to its biophysical environment to guarantee adequate food and shelter for the population. Technology plays a key role here. The second imperative is *political*, the need to develop mechanisms for collective decision-making, goal attainment, and conflict resolution. The political apparatus of societies grows progressively more complex, something we realize when we think of the difference between the systems of headmen, of tribal chiefs, of kings, and of the governments of modern states. The third imperative involves *integration*, the formation of what Parsons calls "the societal community," the strengthening of the population's loyalty to that particular society as a whole over other conflicting loyalties—either to other societies or to subgroups, such as clans, within the society. The fourth imperative Parsons characterizes as "*fiduciary*," the maintenance of a strong value-system and the corresponding attitude of trust in the society's members. The primary social function of religion is fiduciary.

The definition of structural differentiation speaks of multifunctional systems and systems with specific functions. Social systems involve interacting individuals oriented to a common situation in terms of cultural symbols. A multifunctional system is one grouping of individuals whose common work has several social functions. Take, for example, the headman system in hunting and gathering and some horticultural societies. The headman enacted political, economic, and religious roles. Specialist roles in these spheres did not exist. Gradually, however, these different functions came to be performed by different individuals and groupings. The development of a more extensive division of labor with the agricultural revolution meant full-time specialists. In medieval Europe, the beginning of secularization can be seen in the differentiation of the church and the state. The king had powers in the secular sphere, while the archbishops and clergy had authority in the spiritual sphere. This meant a separation of political authority and moral "fiduciary" authority, a development with advantages and disadvantages for the society.

Structural differentiation was hastened by the industrial revolution. Until the nineteenth century, the extended kinship group combined economic, political, integrative, and fiduciary roles. Since agricultural work was a family enterprise, the male family head had a role of economic authority as the task leader of the farming process, had a role of political authority as the clan leader, and had integrative and fiduciary roles as "good citizen" and religious exemplar. The medieval craft guilds found in the cities were also family affairs, thus combining economic and "familial" functions. Even the early "industrial" production of cotton cloth under the "putting-out" system of cottage industry made economic production a function of the family. However, shifting this production to factories meant the severing of the family's economic function. Economic organizations fulfilled the economic function, governmental bureaucracies came to assume the political function, and families had a more limited role involving the integrative function of socialization of children as "upstanding" members of the society and the fiduciary (or "pattern-maintenance" in Parsons's earlier formulation) function of inspiring trust and providing emotional succor.

A crucial aspect of structural differentiation is the development of *relative autonomy* for the institutional sectors: the economy, the polity (political organizations and government), the family, and organized religion. The autonomy of the institutional sectors has its roots in the adaptation process central to social evolution. So long as the institutional sectors are tightly controlled by a central value-system, which historically was religious in character, the institutional sectors are restricted in their capacity to respond to adaptive challenges in the society's environment. The classic case is the religious prohibition against charging interest (usury) in medieval Europe. This norm impeded the development of the economy by preventing the formation of capital. The maneuverability of the institutional sectors is increased by the relaxation of central control. Each of the institutional sectors is said to have "a logic of its own" and its leaders want the freedom to follow that logic without undue restriction.

German sociologist Niklas Luhmann (1982) emphasizes the importance of the autonomy of institutional realms for the stability of complex modern societies. If these realms were not autonomous, environmental changes affecting one sector would automatically impact all the sectors. Luhmann contends that autonomy provides security against even more wrenching social change than we are presently experiencing.

Nevertheless, structural differentiation and the growing autonomy of institutional realms have had dramatic effects on the social psychological situation of modern people.[7] Continual wrenching mental shifts are required as individuals move through the days and weeks, going from the home environment oriented to "family values" to a job situation dominated by economic values to a civic interest group meeting reflecting the political culture to church worship on Sunday exemplifying a religious perspective. Such pluralistic experiences have had obvious unsettling effects on what people take for granted as established reality and truth.

Secularization

We hear our modern time in history continually referred to as a secular age. Secularization can be defined as a shrinkage in the role of religion, both in social life and in individual consciousness (Berger 1974). The shrinkage of religion's sphere represents a distinctive feature of *modern* pluralism, since traditional civilizations (the Roman Empire at the time of Jesus, for example) often manifested a pluralism of religious viewpoints.

When we define secularization as a shrinkage in the role of religion in social life and individual consciousness, there is an ambiguity in this definition as Peter Berger (1974, 132) points out. Does it mean that people have fewer religious experiences in modern secularized societies? If so, then we would be talking about a change in human consciousness. Does it mean that modern people have religious experiences but are not allowed to talk about them? If the latter is true, we are speaking about the *delegitimation* of religious experience. "Religious experience, so to speak, would be hidden in brown paper wrappers" (1974, 132). Berger believes this second meaning of secularization is more true than the first.

Pastoral care confronts the personal stress caused by the delegitimation of religious experience. We see this tension in the case of Allen, a sixty-nine-year-old retired accountant. Allen is hospitalized in a coronary care unit for his second heart attack in less than two years. The hospital chaplain learns about Allen from his children who are assembled in the family waiting room.

A son tells the chaplain how the family is concerned that their father has somehow lost the will to live. "Dad was making a good physical recovery from his earlier heart attack, but he continued to seem so depressed to us." Later, the chaplain has two conversations with Allen.

These conversations reveal a striking dilemma in Allen's definition of his situation. One side of the dilemma is this man's spiritual experience. Allen told the chaplain how his wife of forty-two years had died of cancer three years earlier. The patient showed strong emotion when talking about his love for her and how he missed her. He reported that he often went to his wife's grave. "I feel like we communicate with each other," he said. Asked how that was, Allen became choked with emotion and could not explain. The chaplain believed Allen had a sense of mystical encounter with his wife. Later in this conversation, Allen spoke about a "delusion" he had been gripped by; the chaplain understood it to be a visionary experience. Though hostile to organized religion, Allen also described a significant conversation with a church pastor.

The other side of Allen's dilemma is his strongly rationalistic and empirically oriented worldview. This perspective came out when the chaplain asked him about his beliefs concerning death.

CHAPLAIN: What about death? Do you think there's an afterlife?
ALLEN: All I *know* is what is right here. You and me and this life. All the rest is speculation.
CHAPLAIN: Do you think that you and your wife will be reunited?
ALLEN: I just don't know. I know people with strong faith and beliefs but that's not me.

Allen's strong this-worldly rationalism affected his attitude toward the future. Although the crisis period of his heart attack was behind him, he worried about a minor medical procedure that his physician recommended.

CHAPLAIN: Do you feel as if you're jinxed? Other people could go through this all right but not you?
ALLEN: No, not that, but one problem seems to lead to two more. We talk about "quality of life." My first heart attack knocked a lot of strength out of me. The doctors said I was making a good recovery but it didn't feel that way to me. Now I've been hit hard again. The way I look at it, my wife and I had good years together, I feel that I made a contribution through

> my years of work, but now what further contribution to society can I make?
>
> CHAPLAIN: You're really questioning the meaning of your life at this point.
>
> ALLEN: Yes, and the possibility of enjoying more years. If I could travel, go out for coffee like I used to with my friends, have strength for these things, that would be real life for me. But the future doesn't look good.
>
> CHAPLAIN: It sounds like you feel that unless your life can be really good, you don't want to deal with the trouble and the difficulty.
>
> ALLEN: That is an understatement!
>
> CHAPLAIN: Is it true that since your wife died, you have been struggling to find a meaning for your life?
>
> ALLEN: I guess that's right.
>
> CHAPLAIN: You know, lots of people who come to this hospital for physical problems of one kind or another have underlying spiritual conflicts which trouble them very deeply. Our modern age doesn't encourage us to think about spiritual problems.
>
> ALLEN: That's very true. What happens when you talk with people who have spiritual conflicts like you say?

Allen has articulated a crucial modern "sociology of knowledge" problem, the inadequacy of a secular, rationalistic worldview to handle the multiple levels of his experienced reality. Religious experience was delegitimated for this man, whose theory of knowledge ("All I *know* is right here") demanded a scientific, empirical test of every element of his consciousness. His worldview is a veritable Procrustean bed, cutting off a deeply significant part of his experience. At this point, the conversation became a discussion of alternative definitions of the situation and the implications of a religious understanding of his situation.

Secularization, insofar as it represents a delegitimation of religious experience, is cognitive reductionism. The characteristic mentality of modernism rejects the multiple levels of reality and advances unidimensional worldviews.[8] The religious mode of consciousness, as we saw in Schutz's analysis, is denied truth value. Only "this-worldly" experience is understood as real knowledge. Reality not readily testable by scientific methods is consigned to a quasitruth status of "speculation."

The sociology of knowledge illuminates the problem of the reality-assumptions of careseekers' cognitive worlds. The pastoral caregiver, by standing *outside* the individual's cognitive world, asks what modes of consciousness may be denied legitimacy. When any mode of consciousness is delegitimized, it does not go away, but rather it creates a condition of cognitive dissonance. The components of the careseeker's mental world do not fit; hence the disturbance and strain.

Pastoral care explores with the careseeker the possibility of the religious definition of the situation. Here we hold before the care-seeker the astounding realization that definitions of the situa-tion—being selective perceptions—are choices we make in understanding our world and our experience. The sociology of knowledge dethrones the reigning cognitive "monarch"—the modernist mentality—and opens the possibility for modern ratio-nal people seriously to consider the religious perspective.

Plausibility Structures

Berger and Luckmann make this unqualified assertion in *The Social Construction of Reality*: "Religion requires a religious com-munity, and to live in a religious world requires affiliation with that community" (1966, 158). Belief-systems require confirming social interactions to have stability and viability. The complex of social interactions that reinforce a worldview constitutes what Berger and Luckmann call its *plausibility structure*. The function of the social mechanisms comprising the plausibility structure is reality-maintenance.

It is useful here to think of an analogy between reality-maintenance and hot-air balloons. Belief-systems are like the "en-velope" or balloon part of a hot-air balloon. The social mechanisms that constitute the plausibility structure for a belief-system can be likened to the burner. The hot-air balloon only stays aloft as long as the burner fires blasts of hot gas into the envelope. Likewise, the social rituals of our daily encounters with other people are the "burners" that support the "envelope" of our worldviews.

Supporting the key "knowledge" of a society, its central definitions of reality, are standard behaviors of its members, the total
complex of which is the plausibility structure. These behaviors—
approving and disapproving reactions—maintain the boundary
around what that society considers real, true, and plausible. It
happens that communication with the dead, a phenomenon
hinted at by Allen in the conversation, is an example Berger and
Luckmann use. Communication with the dead in traditional societies had high plausibility, its reality being confirmed by language
and approving social interactions. In modern society, outside
some occult circles, communication with the dead is regarded as
highly implausible, and its practitioners are recommended for
psychiatric evaluations. A complex of social sanctions, in other
words a plausibility structure, rewards "proper" definitions of reality and punishes "deviant" definitions.

Worldview and Ethos

Clifford Geertz (1966) offers a particularly incisive analysis of
the link between worldviews and their supporting social mechanisms in his comparative studies of religion. *Worldviews* are cognitive beliefs about cosmic order and reality, while the social
mechanisms of reality-maintenance he calls a people's *ethos*, their
way of life, which has cathectic (emotion, affect, feeling, aesthetic)
and evaluative (moral) aspects. A symbol system that represents
the structure of reality (for example, a cosmology, a scientific theory) is a model *of* reality, Geertz asserts, whereas a symbol system
whose purpose is to manipulate reality is a model *for* reality. Religious symbols are both models *of* reality and models *for* reality at
the same time. To say that God is love (worldview) is also to say
that the way of love (ethos) governs people's behavior. The two
kinds of models strengthen each other, the cognitive model *of* reality providing an objective authority for the way of life, and the
model *for* reality, how one feels and acts as a believer, gives emotional and moral authority to the worldview. We say, in effect, the
objective cosmos (worldview) must be such-and-so because we
experience these corresponding subjective moods and motiva-
tions (ethos).

Geertz establishes this link between worldview and ethos in his
well-known definition of religion.

> A religion is (1) a system of symbols which acts to (2) establish powerful, pervasive, and long-lasting moods and motivations in men by (3) formulating conceptions of a general order of existence and (4) clothing these conceptions with such an aura of factuality that (5) the moods and motivations seem uniquely realistic. (1966, 4)

In other words, a religious symbol system acts as a model *for* reality, generating powerful emotions and moral sentiments by positing a model *of* reality, a picture of cosmic order. Although this model *of* reality, the worldview, is nonempirical and cannot be proven by normal everyday investigation, people engage in community activities that establish the worldview as "really real," so that the way of life—the people's ethos—has a subjective feeling of total rightness.

How is the "aura of factuality" of the religious worldview fostered? This is the job of ritual. Geertz speaks of religious ritual as "consecrated behavior."

> The acceptance of authority that underlies the religious perspective that the ritual embodies thus flows from the enactment of the ritual itself. By inducing a set of moods and motivations—an ethos—and defining an image of cosmic order—a world-view—by means of a single set of symbols, the performance makes the model *for* and the model *of* aspects of religious belief mere transpositions of one another. (1966, 34)

Through ritual, we get a sense of the religious worldview as "really real" and of the ethos as "uniquely realistic."

Summing Up

The sociology of knowledge deals with the social process of selective perception. Its foundational concept is the definition of the situation, the interpretation step between stimulus and response. A society's culture is the total of its accepted definitions of the situation. The modern pluralistic situation—because it disrupts people's experience of an established "taken-for-granted" symbolic universe, is both enticing and threatening. Unheard of choices and freedoms become possible, yet the old sureties and traditional patterns can no longer give security.

Modern consciousness represents one of the several historic

modes of consciousness. Because this dominant consciousness is a complex of selective perceptions, people's awareness and sensitivity of certain realities is heightened and their recognition of other realities is obscured. The experience of religious reality loses out in the modern cognitive world to the primacy of other realities. The sociology of knowledge challenges the assumptions of modernism and demands the full recognition of the multiple levels of reality.

The sociology of knowledge has two interests, the different modes of consciousness or worldviews and the social mechanisms that support these modes of consciousness. The growing appreciation of a systemic understanding of pastoral care makes caregivers very conscious how careseekers' new definitions of the situation are unstable without social support in their systems. Here we begin to explore the *implications* of a religious definition of the situation. Religious viewpoints are precarious unless reinforced by a careseeker's social interaction patterns.

3. The Individual, Community, and Society In Pastoral Care

The sociology of knowledge, as we saw in the last chapter, alerts pastoral caregivers to the social interactions that support careseekers' worldviews. These interactions constitute the worldviews' plausibility structures. Allen, the cardiac patient, lacked a plausibility structure that could give legitimacy to his religious experiences. His associates, largely professional men like him, reinforced an empirical, "scientific," this-worldly worldview that was inadequate to handle his experience of reality.

The modern society differs markedly from the traditional society in regard to the social mechanisms supporting people's worldviews. In the traditional society, the *total* social experience—all social interactions—reinforced a common worldview. In modern society, made up of a congeries of groups and communities with different values, a person's plausibility structure is no longer the total social experience but is rather a set of interactions within a particular group context *chosen by the individual.* The group whose definition of the situation constitutes a plausibility structure for the person's worldview is called her or his *reference group.* There are many possible reference groups available in the pluralistic society, and the one we choose as *ours* has major implications for our self-identity.

Pastoral care, as the exploration with careseekers of the possibility and implications of religious definitions of their situation, is crucially involved with the dynamics of reference group behavior and the resulting social identity. Alternative definitions of the situation have their anchorage in different reference groups. Whatever term we use for the transformation that careseekers experience in pastoral care—growth, maturation, liberation, consciousness-raising, integration—this change involves new definitions of the situation and new reference groups.

This chapter focuses on the distinctive character of reference group behavior and identity formation in the modern society characterized by massive cultural pluralism. The discussion will put us squarely in the heart of the debate about "individualism" in pastoral care. A strong criticism of contemporary pastoral care concerns its alleged encouragement of individualism. This critique applies broadly to pastoral care, psychology, and modern therapeutic counseling in general. According to the critics, these therapeutic modalities, by emphasizing the self, personal growth, and self-actualization, undermine commitment to others, social bonds, and community involvement.

This chapter develops the thesis that the "individualism" debate has been framed in such a way as to distort the issue. Sociologists tend to start with the society and subordinate the individual to its imperatives, whereas psychologists have focused on the individual's needs and view the society as repressive and constraining. The two disciplines thus talk past each other. The mediating position, which orients this chapter, grows out of the symbolic interactionist tradition of social psychology.

The Social Self

The pioneer of reference group theory was George Herbert Mead. Mead (1962) developed the idea of the "social self," which sheds light on the complex interaction between the individual and the group in the formation of the self-concept. Parallel understandings of this interaction are found in Freud,[1] Durkheim, and American sociologist Charles Horton Cooley. Certain distinctive ideas in Mead's formulation, however, caused his conception to become the central orientation for the symbolic interactionist school of social psychology.

The social self for Mead has two phases. The first phase is "self-consciousness." It is formed as the individual takes the standpoint of the others in the group and views herself or himself through their eyes. Kohlberg and Gilligan quote a child who describes this process:

> You have to like dream that your mind leaves your body and goes into the other person, then it comes back into you and you

see it like he does and you act like the way you saw it from
there. (Quoted in R. Coser 1991, 8)

The child who looks at herself from the mother's position and
says, "Oh, I'm a good girl" (or a "naughty girl" depending on
the circumstances), illustrates Mead's self-consciousness. A baseball game, a favorite illustration Mead uses, is a complex definition of the situation, and each player conceives his or her own
role by understanding the perspectives of all the other players
toward that position. Self-consciousness, Mead says, "refers to
the ability to call out in ourselves a set of definite responses
which belong to the others of the group" (1962, 163). For example, we learn to use a word to influence the actions of others, but
using that word, we generate in ourselves the same attitude it
evokes in others. Thinking about an action thus becomes an *internal conversation.* Suppose we start to say something, but then
we react to what we plan to say by taking the role of the other
("that's really a cruel thing to say"), and we don't say it. We try
out another action and go through the same process. Thus standing outside ourselves to take an "objective" view of ourselves
generates one phase of the human self, "self-consciousness," or
what Mead calls the "Me."

A pastoral situation will clarify this idea of thinking as an internal conversation where we take the role of the other. The charge
nurse of a hospital unit made a pastoral care referral of a cancer
patient whom his primary nurse reported to be "depressed." I had
various options in how to approach the patient. Mentally, I "tried
on" various "presentations of self." I could begin the conversation, "Hello, I'm so-and-so, one of the chaplains. Mrs. Smith, this
unit's charge nurse, asked me to visit you." Taking the role of the
patient, I expected his natural question to be, "Why does she think
I need to see a chaplain?" In response, I would have been forced
to say something like, "Because she thinks you may be depressed." Then the patient, in reply, might ask, "What makes her
think that?" or he could say, "That's total nonsense. Me, depressed? And what does she know about how I feel, anyway?"
Watching this scenario unfold in my mind, I decided from a strategic point of view that I wanted to avoid, in that particular situation, explaining the other staff member's rationale for making the
referral. I chose to use a different "presentation of self": the chaplain doing rounds and "happening by" to see how the patient is

doing. This was somewhat unusual for me, however, because my usual "style" is to be direct and make it clear at the outset when my visit comes from a referral.

If the first phase of the social self is self-consciousness, the "Me," then the other phase is reaction and assertion, Mead's "I." Human beings are not thralls or slaves of society. Self-consciousness, the "Me," does not determine how we react. The "I" reacts to the self that is formed through taking the attitudes of others. The sense of freedom and initiative humans feel derives from the reality of choice in our reactions. As Mead stresses, there is always an element of uncertainty in how any given person will respond to a situation. Mead's baseball player may make a brilliant play or make an error. My approach to the cancer patient that particular day was not my usual style, and thus it was surprising to me. Social innovation and asocial behavior are just as much the result of the "I" aspect of the self as well-socialized conformist behavior.

The self in symbolic interactionist theory is thus a two-phase social process, alternating between the role-taking phase, Mead's "Me," and the choice-making phase, his "I." The implication of this perspective, necessarily presented here in a simplified form, is quite profound. As one of Mead's leading students, sociologist Herbert Blumer (1969), points out, the two-phase model of self exposes an important limitation of systems theory for understanding social interrelationships. Systems theory is based on mechanistic models: If A does X, then B reacts by doing Y, thus causing A to perform act Z. Symbolic interactionist theory, by introducing the uncertainty and freedom of the choice-making "I" phase, eliminates the determinacy of systems models. Clearly there is a systemic aspect to human social interaction, but its actual expression always hinges on the autonomous and unpredictable initiatives of the actors.

Mead developed a conception of self-identity from his perspective on the social self. There is a consistency of self through time, maintained in the different group settings involving a person. To explain this consistency of self-consciousness, Mead formulated the concept of the "generalized other," a mental synthesis of the attitudes of other people. This idea helped him explain why people are not highly nervous every time they shift social settings or meet new people.

The idea of people forming a "generalized other" has greatest applicability to relatively homogenous societies. In pluralistic, societies, where many groups and communities with different values and perspectives compete, it is more difficult to speak of persons constructing the "generalized other." Here sociologists and social psychologists observe the process whereby individuals orient themselves to *significant others*, those particular persons who constitute the individual's reference group.

Reference Group

Tamotsu Shibutani (1961, 257) defines a reference group as "that group, real or imaginary, whose standpoint is being used as the frame of reference by the actor." The frame of reference is another way of speaking about the actor's definition of the situation. Those frames or definitions are anchored in the cultures of groups. Reference group theory points to the important fact of modern society that individuals choose their definition of the situation, and this choice depends upon the group with which they choose to identify. The traditional society, with its lack of pluralism, afforded limited choice of identities or group standpoints.

One's reference group may be a group to which he or she belongs, or it may be a group to which the individual aspires to belong, or it may be a group that would be forever closed to that particular person's membership, or as Shibutani observes, it may be an imaginary group. Upward social mobility, in which someone moves to a higher socioeconomic status, often involves a person raised in a working-class environment adopting the values and perspective of the middle class before gaining entrance to a middle-class occupation. Sociologists call this "anticipatory socialization." The self-hatred of ethnic minority people is also an example of reference group behavior. An African-American, Asian-American, or Jewish-American person adopts the standpoint of white Anglo Saxons toward their own racial characteristics. Consequently, these ethnic people come to perceive their natural characteristics (kinky hair, slanted eyes, prominent noses) as stigmas. Campaigns like "black is beautiful" aim to change reference group behavior.

Anton T. Boisen (1928) used reference group theory to understand pastoral care. Earlier it was noted that Boisen was a sociologist, as well as a psychologist of religion. His sociological perspective has received little attention. As an introduction to reference group dynamics, we will look at Boisen's theory of reference groups and individual psychopathology. The influence of George Herbert Mead, John Dewey, and sociologist Lester F. Ward can be discerned in Boisen's sociology.

The key to mental health, Boisen held, is "socializing the difficulty." The meaning of this phrase is spelled out in Boisen's article in the *American Journal of Sociology*, "The Sense of Isolation in Mental Disorders: Its Religious Significance" (January 1928). This article is a case analysis of two teenage brothers, one of whom is seen by a psychiatrist, Dr. William Healy. The identified patient in this family is a boy who is brought before the juvenile court for stealing. The parents report that the boy shows neurotic symptoms at home: restlessness, irritability, inability to eat, and nausea. The other brother is described as quiet, honest, good-spirited, and well adjusted.

Both boys a year or two before had encounters with another boy who introduced them to vulgar language and stealing. The "neurotic" brother found the vulgarity totally upsetting. He could never say those words. When the obscene words came into his mind, he thought about the boy who used them, and then he thought about stealing. He did not feel stealing was half as bad as the sexual vulgarity, and he began stealing and found he could get away with it.

The "healthy" brother had become accustomed to using the vulgarity, thinking nothing of it. He got in the habit of tormenting his sibling at the dinner table by whispering the distressing words to him. The latter's inability to eat and his nausea seem related to the "healthy" brother's needling.

In his analysis of these youths' situation, Boisen contrasts how the two boys dealt with inner conflict. The "healthy" brother socializes the experience of the vulgar words, finding peers who share the same interests. He lowers his standards a bit but remains frank and unconflicted within. The "neurotic" brother becomes isolated, maintaining his sense of self-respect (he refuses to say those vulgar words) at the cost of feeling dirty and unfit for the company of his family and perceiving himself as different from his peers. His stealing is a way to deal with the stress of his conflict.

Boisen holds that the inability to socialize and thus assimilate the evil or difficulty is the primary factor in mental illness.[2]

> It is probably safe to say that no man will have mental disorder so long as he can feel himself an integral part of some group whose standards he is able to accept as final. (1928, 557)

Boisen identifies a number of psychological reactions that serve to preserve the person's self-respect at the cost of isolation: compromise, diversion, bluffing, shifting responsibility, and withdrawal.

> All these methods serve to encyst the evil and to conceal it from one's self and thus to preserve one's self-respect. But the result is isolation. A man thus becomes queer, odd, different from his fellows not merely in their eyes but first of all in his own. (1928, 560)

It is significant, Boisen asserts, that acute psychotic disturbance and psychoanalysis have the same function: bringing the cause of the difficulty from the realm of evasion and concealment into the clear light of consciousness. Acute psychotic episodes may or may not lead to psychic integration. Some such experiences have the character of religious conversions and can lead to healing.

Psychoanalysis socializes the difficulty; the psychiatrist hears the terrible things and does not condemn, and thus the sufferer feels forgiven and restored to right relationship with society. (This oversimplifies Boisen's analysis of the psychiatric relationship, for he discusses transference and other psychoanalytic concepts.)

Boisen distinguishes two modes of socializing evil and difficulty, what we might call "downward" and "upward." The "healthy" brother socialized his difficulty downward; in Boisen's terms, he "socialized his inferiorities." Groups rationalize their weaknesses and immorality; they use protective devices to defend the group's moral self-respect. Socrates' hemlock and Jesus' cross were the cost they bore for threatening the moral self-respect of groups socializing their inferiorities. The other alternative is to socialize the evil upward, developing an integration with the highest possibilities of human society, as represented in the church (at its best) and prophetic people like Paul of Tarsus, George Fox, and John Bunyan.

The differentiation between the physician and psychiatrist, on the one hand, and the religious worker on the other, lies right here. Physicians and psychiatrists seem content with socializing "downward" where the "normal" is synonymous with "average." The goal of therapy is the prevention of unrest and disorder. The religious worker strives to socialize evil upward. In Boisen's words,

> [his] attention must ever be centered upon "the vast realm of unattained possibility" and whose constant aim must be to bring himself into right relationship with the friendly and protective forces of the universe for the attainment of the possibilities of which he has become aware. (1928, 567)

Here Boisen sounds the theme of Lester Ward and other turn-of-the-century social Darwinists who, unlike individualistic William Graham Sumner, saw societal evolution happening through planned social cooperation. This Progressive movement theme comes through strongly in Boisen's two final sentences: The ultimate test is the biological test, the test of

> survival, stated, however, not in terms of the individual but in terms of society and social values. Therefore, we say that the truly happy solution is one which results in progressive unification with the abiding and universal elements in human society. (1928, 567)

To sum up, Boisen presents a sociological model of mental health focused on the relationship between the individual and the society. Figure 3-1 represents the logic of Boisen's analysis. The various communities comprising the society have different moral standards. At Time 1, individuals confront evil and difficulty, as when the two boys associated with their profane peer. At Time 2, one of three choices has been made. One is not to socialize the evil, that is, to identify with the standards of a morally "high" community and to conceal sinful impulses. This choice leads to mental illness. A second option is to socialize the evil downward, that is, to identify with the standards of a "low" community and to be open about those impulses. This choice yields "average" mental health but group behaviors that are often morally questionable. The third option involves socializing the evil upward, where persons identify with a "high" community, admit publicly that they have sinful impulses, then experience forgiveness and reconciliation, and continue to aspire toward the higher possibilities embodied in the "high" community's standards. This choice represents the healthy religious option.

The logic of Boisen's analysis suggests that the three options are open again at Time 3 for the individual. The mentally ill person may continue not to socialize the evil. That person may, however, succeed in socializing the evil and achieve some degree of mental health. Psychoanalysis allows for the experience of forgiveness and acceptance, Boisen holds, but often compromises moral standards in the process, thus socializing the evil downward. Pastoral care, on the other hand, aids persons in socializing evil upward, yielding religiously oriented mental health.

The reference group perspective is central to Boisen's analysis. First, identification with one reference group over another is a choice of the individual. The situation for both brothers, not only in their family but also in exposure to the deviant behavior of vulgarity and theft, was similar. The boys made different choices in responding to an essentially similar situation. Second, the reference group choices had major implications for their psychological condition. As we know from the Thomas theorem, definitions of the situation have real social and psychological consequences.

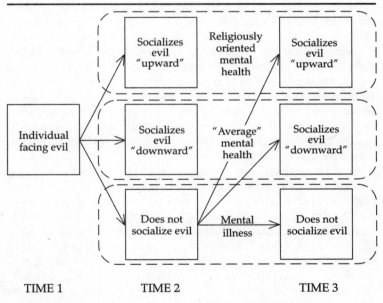

FIG. 3-1. Reference group behavior and mental health
in Anton Boisen's case study

Third, therapeutic modalities work with reference group orientations. Standards of adequacy—social, ethical, and religious—
operate in the therapeutic milieu, defining what "health" means.

Thus in this case and analysis from the 1920s, we see an early
application by a pastoral caregiver of reference group theory to a
therapeutic situation. As we will see in the next section, reference
group theory is crucial to understanding the identity of careseekers in pastoral care.

Identity

Reference groups and identity are integrally related. Conceiv-
ing of the social self as having the two phases of "Me" and "I," the
self-consciousness derived from taking the role of others toward
oneself depends on *which* others those are, or *which* reference
group. Self-consciousness anchored in a particular reference
group is the basis for part of the individual's identity, the *social
identity*. The "I," the assertive, initiating, autonomous reaction
constitutes the basis for the other part of self-identity, the *personal
identity*.

Symbolic interactionist John Hewitt (1989, 149–90) distinguishes four elements of identity. *Continuity* is the feeling that
one's experience of self makes temporal sense. *Integration* is the
feeling of wholeness that comes from sensing a fit between the different social roles and interpersonal roles one assumes. *Identification* is the sense of social solidarity one has with others in one's
group or culture. *Differentiation* is the sense of the boundaries between the self and others.

Social behavior is always understood as enacted before some
audience. This is a central tenet of sociologists such as Erving
Goffman (1959), who espouse a dramaturgical understanding of
society. Reference group theory poses the question, What people
comprise the audience for the social actor's performance? Modernity creates new possibilities for how the individual defines his or
her "audience." Today's increase in range of communication, geographical mobility, the spread of mass media, and the pluralization of life-worlds create the possibility for modern people to
choose as their reference group or "audience" not the immediate
neighborhood or community but rather the whole society or
world. To encompass this possibility, Robert Merton (1957,

387–420) distinguishes two types of reference group orientation: the "locals" and the "cosmopolitans." Locals feel comfortable in the intimate face-to-face relationships of the small town or the urban neighborhood. The close community of family, church congregation, neighbors, and townspeople represents their "world." Locals are part of the town "grapevine" and gravitate toward the "homey" local newspaper and the gossip circuit. Cosmopolitans live in a different "world," where national and international events are the significant "news." Rather than enjoying a small-town newspaper, they thrive on *The New York Times.* Their occupations are often professional and managerial and involve communication with comparably placed people in distant areas. An educational difference often, but not always, distinguishes locals and cosmopolitans, the latter tending to have university and postgraduate training.

John Hewitt (1989) distinguishes the person's social identity and his or her personal identity. The social identity grows out of the community contexts of the individual's life. Social identity begins in the family and develops in school, work, and other community settings. The organic community of small-town and face-to-face relationships encourages the development of the social identity. One's social identity reflects Mead's "Me," the conventionalized aspect of one's self. Personal identity, on the other hand, is based on the self and its projects, not the community and its expectations. It stresses differentiation from others, not identification with them. The "stage" upon which the actor "performs" his or her life is deemed the larger society, not the smaller communities. Personal identity stresses the "I," the active, innovative, nonconformist part of one's self. Everyone has both a social identity and a personal identity. People vary, however, in the relative importance of these two identities. Moreover, different social eras encourage greater emphasis on one or the other. The modern period emphasizes personal identity. And the struggle between psychology and sociology has reflected the former's greater attention to personal identity—the self breaking free of social constraints—and the latter's greater attention to social identity—the power of class, race, and socialization as determining factors in people's behavior.

Hewitt (1989, 191–230) analyzes the dilemmas of the American self in terms of the choice modern people face between emphasizing social identity and personal identity. For Americans, this dilemma goes back in their history to the decision about migration: to stay or to leave? Staying in one geographical spot meant accepting the social identity and the constraints of the existing community. Leaving meant seeking a personal identity that was future-oriented and revolved around the personal project, the new self one hoped to build.

Hewitt distinguishes three strategies of self-construction. The "exclusivist" strategy stresses social identity in the quasi-communities available today: small-town life, more conservative religious groups, associational communities of one kind or another. The key here is to feel total oneness with the group and to experience keenly the boundaries between this group and the rest of the society. The social identity is paramount, and the strictness of the group and the strong norms about group loyalty are accepted as the price one pays for the benefits of close fellowship.[3]

The "autonomy" strategy represents the opposite extreme from the exclusivistic strategy. Here the strong emphasis is on the personal project, on differentiation rather than identification. Modern society creates the possibility of viewing one's life on the stage of "society" rather than the "community."

The "pragmatic" strategy rejects both extremes. This is the path most people take. Here the values of identification and differentiation are given relatively equal weight. There is a sense of role distance here, the idea of being in community but not totally absorbed by it. One lives in the middle, feeling the value of community, but sensing the problem of too-close ties; experiencing the value of autonomy and the freedom of creating one's own special life, yet rejecting the extreme of too-great autonomy, sensing the need for social ties.

This dilemma of identification versus differentiation poses a basic struggle for careseekers in pastoral care. The family systems approach oriented to Murray Bowen's strong emphasis on differentiation needs the corrective of the dual orientation from Mead's social psychology. Clearly our careseekers are ambivalent, seeking self-identity that expresses *both* identification and differentiation. Using this social-psychological perspective of reference groups and identity, we now analyze specifically the dynamics of the religious congregation.

Meaning and Community

A plausibility structure for the religious worldview is a reference group. We saw in chapter 2 that worldview and ethos are closely linked. In the modern pluralistic society, the total social experience does not provide reality maintenance for the religious worldview. This function must be performed by particular communities of faith. For Christians, the churches fulfill this role. If worldview and ethos are associated, we would expect that church participation generates stronger religious conviction.

Research on religious affiliation demonstrates the importance of reference group orientation as an intervening variable between church participation and religious belief, between community and meaning. Wade Clark Roof, a sociologist of religion, studied the dynamics of church congregational life in terms of reference group behavior. This investigation is reported in his important book, *Community and Commitment: Religious Plausibility in a Liberal Protestant Church* (1978). This rich study is based on a carefully drawn sample of North Carolina Episcopalians.

A major finding of the Episcopal survey is that the local church represents a plausibility structure supporting religious worldviews *only for some church members*. Here we would think that the degree of church participation would influence the strength of the member's religious orientation. The more church members attend church and are exposed to the preaching and teaching, the more their transcendent belief-system will be reinforced. This expectation turns out to be true, but only for the church members who are, using Merton's types of reference group orientation, *locals*. For cosmopolitans, those people with a national or an international perspective, there is little if any association between the belonging indicators and the meaning indicators. Putting this another way, the orthodoxy of the religious belief system of a church member who qualifies as a *local* is directly related to how regular that person is in church attendance, how active in other church activities and in congregational friendships. For church members who are *cosmopolitans*, the same is not true. How orthodox they are shows no relationship to their level of church participation. What is the implication of this? Cosmopolitans have lower orthodoxy (transcendental religion) scores than locals. Among the cosmopolitans, church activity level has little to do with how orthodox they are, but among the locals, it has a lot to do with orthodoxy. In short, only those persons oriented to the local church as a primary group and *as a reference group* will derive greater support for their religious beliefs by increasing participation in the local church.

Roof (1978, 156–57) asked several pastoral-care type questions in the Episcopal survey, including a set of questions about how the death of a relative or close friend affected the respondent's religious faith. Deaths are probably the most shattering personal experiences with which we must cope, and religion is, of course, the primary resource people use to understand and get through times of loss and bereavement. But deaths and crisis may cause the weakening of religious belief because those beliefs seem to be inadequate to deal with the immensity of the crisis. Respondents were asked if, since they had become an adult, anyone who was very close to them (either a relative or a close friend) had died or been killed. Those who had experienced such a loss were then asked what the effect of this death was on their religious beliefs. Three responses were possible: (1) my religious beliefs were strengthened because of the comfort they gave me during this tragedy; (2) this death had little or no effect on my religious beliefs; (3) my religious beliefs were weakened because I couldn't imagine a loving God allowing this death to happen. Roof found that fewer regular than irregular church attenders reported that the death had weakened their faith. He also found that fewer church members who were locals than those who were cosmopolitan reported that the death weakened their faith. Table 1 shows how the combined effect of church participation and having a local reference group orientation decreased the chance that the church member would report that the death weakened his or her faith.

Roof's finding that reference group orientation mediates the reality-maintenance function of church membership has important implications for pastoral care. Pastoral caregivers oriented sociologically realize that careseekers need group support in order to maintain viable religious definitions of their situation. Participation in a local congregation can be very important as a plausibility structure. However, how much association with a church contributes toward strengthening the careseeker's religious beliefs depends upon that person's reference group orientation. Locals will profit, while cosmopolitans are likely to be "*in* the church but not *of* it."

TABLE 1
Effect of Death of a Relative or Friend in
Weakening Belief by Socioreligious Group Involvement
and Local-Cosmopolitan Orientations, in Percentages

Religious group involvement of respondents	Percentage saying death had weakened belief	
	Locals	Cosmopolitans
Regular church attenders	9	27
Irregular church attenders	22	41

Source: Roof, 1978, 157.

What can be done to support cosmopolitans? The Episcopal survey shows cosmopolitans to be more meaning-oriented in their religious pursuit, the locals to be more belonging-oriented. The
cosmopolitans look more at the theological kernel of Christian belief, whereas the locals accept a larger theological-cultural package.
The cultural conservatism of many locals' religious orientation
turns off a good number of cosmopolitans. If a group context is to
prove meaningful as a plausibility structure for cosmopolitans'
transcendent religion, it needs to be focused on the theological
"nitty-gritty" of the faith, not sociality for the sake of sociality.
Group Bible study and prayer groups have been observed to be effective in helping cosmopolitans both to recognize and grapple
with the modernist issues and to understand the dialectic of scripture and experience.

Loneliness

Hospital chaplains work closely with lonely people. Because elderly people represent a major part of the hospitalized population,
chaplains confront the loneliness of widowed persons or couples
whose children are adults, who live geographically removed from
their families, whose retirement means the loss of the social networks characteristic of occupational involvement, and where
death and ill health reduces their social interaction. Much physical
illness, as psychologist James J. Lynch observes in his important

book, *The Broken Heart: The Medical Consequences of Loneliness* (1977), has roots in disrupted social networks.

The ministry of "presence," so central to pastoral care, is understood as an answer to human loneliness. Theologically, the caregiver plays an incarnational role, "representing" the ever-present companionship of God. Henri Nouwen (1972) gives a dramatic example of the ministry of presence in a central case study of *The Wounded Healer*. The clinical pastoral intern encounters a man who is facing critical surgery alone, without any human companionship. Although a stranger to the man until his pre-surgery visit, the intern had the opportunity to offer himself to this man without family or friends as one human being who would wait for him at the other end of his surgery and thus inspire the patient's hope.

Hospital pastoral care today, with increasingly shorter lengths of stay, is involved in discharge planning with church parishes, where the churches agree to provide basic social services to the homecoming patient for the first weeks after hospital discharge. Customarily the immediate family—spouses, daughters, other relatives—or close friends provided this social support, but today we find increasingly that elderly folk lack social networks. Churches pick up the slack. Pastors play a vital role in the coordination of these services. Meals are prepared, light housekeeping is done, transportation to the doctor is provided. Chaplains work with medical social workers in making these contacts with pastors and church parish workers. Hospice programs, with volunteers who provide emotional support for terminally ill patients and their spouses in the home, are another social network for loneliness.

The following case illustrates the dynamics of loneliness, mental health, reference groups, and coordinated hospital and parish pastoral care. Joyce, a seventy-two-year-old woman, had led an isolated life on the outskirts of a smaller metropolitan area. Her parents and uncles had bought a dairy farm and orchard there when Joyce was nine. An only child, she attended a two-room rural high school, then went to business college for a year and was employed in the office of the local Chevrolet dealership. After her marriage, she and her husband, a carpenter, rented a house on the family farmstead, and Joyce terminated her outside employment. The couple was childless, and Joyce's life was focused on her husband, her parents, the orchard, her garden, and her music. Later,

when Joyce's father and uncles died, her mother retained ownership of one home; Joyce and her husband acquired ownership of
the house next door, and the farmland was sold.

Seven years before Joyce's crisis, her by-then-retired husband
had begun manifesting symptoms of Alzheimer's. Two years later,
Joyce's mother developed a serious loss of short-term memory.
Joyce moved her over into her own house, and from then on, Joyce
was occupied around the clock in care for her two mentally impaired loved ones. Finally, upon her doctor's recommendation,
she placed her husband in a nursing home, a decision that caused
her to feel strong guilt. After her husband's death, Joyce felt a big
void in her life and found her way to a small Methodist church in
the area that she had often driven past. A shy person, Joyce appreciated the warm welcome she received from the pastor and the
members. To attend worship, however, Joyce had to fight a continual battle on the home front because of her ninety-year-old
mother's fear of being alone, but finally she was baptized at age
seventy.

Eventually, the stress and exhaustion of caring for the aged
woman reached a crisis point. Joyce had a temporary loss of
speech, and her doctor discovered that her blood pressure was
200/110. By this time, a neighbor woman was coming into Joyce's
home to allow her some time away from the house. Joyce's pastor
had been insistent, telling her, "You need to take some breaks." At
night, Joyce was fearful of going to sleep. At the end of a month of
increasing nervousness, Joyce awoke at 1 A.M. one night in a state
of extreme disturbance. She called a friend down the road, saying,
"Ann, there's something wrong with me." The woman called
Joyce's family doctor, who recommended that Joyce be taken to
the hospital's psychiatric unit. The neighbor and her husband
took Joyce to the hospital and waited with her while she was
being admitted. Joyce directed them to take her mother to a
nearby elderly foster-care home while she was hospitalized.

During her week's hospitalization, Joyce made significant steps
toward reorientation of her isolated life. In addition to daily sessions with a psychiatrist, she participated in therapy groups and
creative activities. In a group led by the unit's chaplain, where life
meaning issues were discussed, Joyce realized that she had
missed a lot of important life experiences. This realization was
pounded home for her when the unit's activity director "ordered"

her to join a group of patients on a recreational outing to a look-out point and ice cream parlor. Surveying the city's lights, Joyce remarked how the city had grown. The activity director asked, "When was the last time you were up here?" Joyce replied that it had been fifty years earlier.

At a treatment team meeting, the staff developed a treatment plan for Joyce. Deciding that Joyce's isolation was the key issue, the team considered ways to structure a larger network of supportive social contacts. Aware of Joyce's church connection and the involvement of her pastor, who visited her every day while she was hospitalized, the chaplain suggested that the patient's permission be sought for the activity therapist to discuss the patient's case with the church pastor and enlist his active involvement. Participation in a community senior center was recommended as part of this plan. While hospitalized, Joyce confronted a central decision, how best to deal with her mother, and decided that it was no longer possible for her to care for her mother at home. Against her mother's strong objection, Joyce realized she would need to put her mother in a nursing home. Emotional support for Joyce as she carried out this difficult decision was also considered a necessary ingredient of the treatment plan.

Joyce entered a new phase of her life with significantly expanding horizons upon her discharge from the hospital. The chaplain recalls how Joyce's "new life" began on her discharge day, when her initial hesitancy changed to obvious excitement over experiencing her first-ever taxicab ride. Joyce's pastor enlisted the cooperation of an assertive church member who, like Joyce, had cared for aged and infirm parents. Her new friend accompanied Joyce when she took her mother to the nursing home and instructed her on how to respond to her mother's resistance. This woman picked up Joyce every Tuesday and Thursday morning for exercise class at the community senior center. She called Joyce every day, planned outings to shops and interesting restaurants, signed them up for bus tours, and skillfully counteracted Joyce's residual inclination to retreat into depressed isolation. Joyce's pastor continued to monitor the implementation of the treatment plan, reporting developments to the hospital activities director.

Joyce began attending a home Bible study in her neighborhood. She discovered a woman who was unable to drive and needed transportation to church and elsewhere. In adult class at church, her pastor watched Joyce develop an openness to new ideas and perspectives. Some months after the crisis of her hospitalization, Joyce reported, "God has blessed me in so many ways through so many people. And I pray that through him, I may be allowed to help others."

Reference group theory is helpful in analyzing situations of loneliness such as Joyce's. Isolation represents a very restricted group of significant others. This woman's "world" was her husband and mother. The larger community psychologically did not exist for her. She did not identify with the larger universe of meaning orienting active elderly persons in her area. The illness and death of her husband and the progressive incapacity of her mother meant that her "world" collapsed. The mental breakdown that brought her to the hospital psychiatric unit signified this. The treatment process "socialized her difficulty," to use Boisen's apt phrase. The chaplain's discussion group became a source of self-consciousness for Joyce, who perceived herself anew through taking the role of the others and discovering how she had missed important life experiences. Through the cooperative work of the activity director, chaplain, and pastor, a new "world" was created for this woman, a community-wide reference group linking church, senior center, and new friends. The chaplain and pastor both reported that Joyce became a new person whose reference group consisted of a notably widened circle of significant others.

Pastoral care is increasingly involved with the formation and leadership of support groups. Twelve-step programs for substance abuse and addiction; support groups for persons with specific illnesses (cancer, diabetes, HIV/AIDS, anorexia-bulimia) and their families; and groups for adult children of alcoholics are some examples. Support groups reorient people's reference group. The assessment of our condition depends on whom we compare ourselves with. Reference group theory makes the critical distinction between absolute deprivation and relative deprivation. The former is a loss defined in objective terms, while the latter involves a comparison between one's loss and the situation of others. Support groups cause persons with a disability, an illness, or a common plight to adopt fellow sufferers as their reference group. Using other impaired persons as their reference group reduces disabled persons' sense of relative deprivation, causing them to have a greater sense of normality about their situation. The extended case study presented in chapter 7 shows in detail how a careseeker's reference group orientation is changed through support groups.

Adult Socialization

Pastoral care, understood sociologically, is a type of adult socialization. We often think of socialization only as the process by which children are changed from human animals to social beings. Yet learning and developing new coping skills are lifelong processes. Socialization is any structured social relationship for the purpose of enhancing learning, coping, and developing new attitudes and perspectives. Pastoral care as defined in this book emphasizes exploration of alternative definitions of the careseeker's situation. When pastoral care does a good job of helping careseekers understand their choices, it facilitates people's learning in a striking way.

Reference group theory is central to a sociological understanding of attitudinal change. The extensive research on people's attitudinal change shows that change in values, perspective, and self-identity does not happen in a social vacuum. The individual's reference group is a key ingredient in successful transformation. We know from studies of rehabilitation of youthful offenders that resocialization fails if young people go right back to their old associates after leaving the rehabilitation program. Only by changing the reference group, and thereby surrounding the individual with people who reward different values and affirm new behaviors, can we expect to see lasting personal transformation.

Seymour Sarason (1971) did an evaluation of a program for training public school teachers in new educational methods. Individual classroom teachers were selected from different schools and sent to a university for the summer to master the new knowledge and skills. They returned in the fall to their separate schools to implement the new methods. Within a brief time, nearly all these teachers had lost enthusiasm for the new methods and had reverted to their old teaching techniques. Sarason discovered that the key factor explaining the failure of the innovation program was its disregard of the local school's staff as the reference group for the newly trained teachers. Their colleagues, not understanding the new methods, were unable to give affirmation and encouragement to them. Only by training a significant portion of a school's staff in the new methods would the teachers have effective social support from a reference group for maintaining the changes (Sarason 1971, cited in Westerhoff and Neville 1974).

Family systems therapy represents a therapeutic application of reference group theory. Reacting to the older individual counseling pattern, its proponents recognize that dysfunctional orientations characterize the interactive pattern of the whole group. Where only one family member undergoes counseling, his or her new attitudes and new behaviors are difficult to sustain in the face of an unaltered reward system in the family setting. Systems therapy aims at resocialization of all system members, thereby transforming the reference group toward which each system member is oriented.

Comparative studies of dyadic and group contexts for attitudinal change show that the one-to-one traditional counseling mode achieves far less effective new learning than group contexts. Early studies by Kurt Lewin, Kurt W. Back, Muzafer Sherif, and Theodore Newcomb documented the greater influence of groups on individuals' attitudes. Bernard Berelson and Gary Steiner sum up the research findings in the following theorem:

> When change is desired, it is typically more effective to influence people as group members than to do so in an isolated, individual-by-individual manner. (1964, 354)

In addition, the greater the cohesiveness of the group, that is, the more group members like being part of the group, the greater is the influence of group decisions on the thinking of each member. Cohesiveness is an indicator of the degree to which group members are "significant others" for the individual, and thus provides a measure of the extent to which the small group represents a reference group for each person.

Understood in terms of reference groups and socialization, Christian pastoral care has a notable kinship with sociologically informed Christian education. John Westerhoff and Gwen Kennedy Neville (1974) make this connection for Protestant Christian education, while Regis Duffy (1983) does the same for Catholic pastoral care. Westerhoff and Neville emphasize the decisive role of reference groups in personal change in the following terms:

> People change when they unite with a community which lives and supports a life style different from their previous style of life. . . .True conversion is not essentially an individualistic act.

It results from contact with a community. Individual conversion
is nothing more than a passing outburst unless it is sustained
within a community. (1974, 151)

Thus Westerhoff and Neville advocate group contexts for pastoral
exploration of life issues.

Obviously, most pastoral care currently uses the one-to-one
structure of individual counseling and conversation. Our institutional roles define how much freedom we have to create and use
group formats. Pastors, chaplains, and pastoral counselors for the
foreseeable future will work in both individual and group settings. What we learn from the sociology of knowledge and social
psychology are some of the advantages of the latter to which we
need to pay greater attention.

Spoiled Identity

Sociologist Erving Goffman in *Stigma: Notes on the Management
of Spoiled Identity* (1963) discusses the situation of persons who are
unable to conform to standards that society calls "normal." The
jacket of this book gives a good overview of his approach:

The physically deformed, the ex-mental patient, the drug addict,
the prostitute, the just plain ugly are constantly forced to adjust
to their precarious social identities—precarious because their
image of themselves must daily confront and be affronted by the
image which others reflect back to them. Dr. Goffman examines
the alternatives which face the stigmatized individual: to display his disability or not to display it; to let on or not let on, to
lie or not to lie; and in each case to whom, when, or where.

Pastoral caregivers support many persons who are stigmatized
and have spoiled identities. Central to the Christian religious
worldview is a redefinition of normality. Caregivers thus offer a
new definition of the situation that erases the dichotomy of stigmatized persons versus normal persons.

Described in traditional Christian terms, persons experience
healing in the Christian community as their spoiled or damaged
identities become transformed into whole ("holy") identities
(Hunter 1979; Smail 1980). The damaged identity results from cultural and human definition, pride in being an exemplary person (a

scribe or a Pharisee) or shame in being an outcast (a tax collector or a prostitute). The whole identity derives from God's definition, a strangely paradoxical identity, every person being simultaneously sinner and redeemed. Healing occurs as the damaged person yields the sin, the alienation, to the dying Jesus on the cross; he or she experiences union with Christ Jesus and thereby as "son" or "daughter" has access to a new relationship with God as "father" or "parent"; and the person's life through the Holy Spirit is progressively transformed to duplicate that of Jesus, reflecting the same sorrow and glory. Confession, forgiving others, sharing the sacraments, praise, intercession, studying scripture, and sacrificial ministry combine into a "way" or lifestyle that sustains the mystical union with Christ and effects ongoing healing in the adherents and powerful prophetic impact on the society. An eschatological orientation pervades the community, an understanding that its obedient life contributes to the fulfillment of God's historical purpose.

Note how reference group theory is involved in conceptualizing the divine-human encounter here, as well as the interpersonal encounter. Mead's "Me" is my perception of my appearance in the eyes of the other. The religious perspective understands the divine-human encounter to be just as real as the human-to-human encounter. From that vantage point, understanding God as part of our social system, taking account of the multiple levels of reality posited by the sociology of knowledge, we take very seriously God as a role partner. Our self-consciousness, therefore, is based significantly on our sense of how God perceives us (Garrett 1979).

Conclusion

This chapter has focused on the concepts of reference group and identity. A basic aspect of pastoral care is dialogue with careseekers exploring alternative definitions of their situation. Reference groups are the social anchorage or "plausibility structure" for definitions of the situation. The personal change or growth occurring through pastoral care involves changes in reference groups. Treating individual psychopathology, working in support groups, building community social networks for careseekers, and managing spoiled identity all involve the restructuring of reference groups and the consequent change of self-identity. Sociology and psychology have talked past each other by neglecting the dual character of the social self—sociology by stressing community, and psychology by emphasizing individual autonomy. Both identification (social identity) and differentiation (personal identity) are important to people, and the problem of self-identity in the modern world involves finding the optimal balance between them.

4. Power, Inequality, and Empowerment in Pastoral Care

This chapter focuses on social stratification and the structures of power in modern society. Key issues facing pastoral care concern power and inequality. Much psychology and family systems therapy largely ignore power. Their ahistorical and astructural approach causes many psychologists and family therapists to neglect the cultural influence of the larger society. The strong critique from radical psychology in the 1960s and from feminist family therapists in the 1980s is centered on the issue of power.

The present chapter provides an introduction to the issue of power, contrasting how this concept is understood in the functionalist and conflict traditions of sociology. The position of the careseeker in the power structure—family, work life, and politics—is a key aspect of his or her problems. Pastoral care needs to be oriented toward the empowerment of careseekers so that they can change their society, not toward adjustment of persons to the existing situation. Chapter 5 continues the examination of power by looking at how religion often is used as an ideological justification for social inequality. Chapter 6 deals with power as it concerns the role conflict experienced by pastoral caregivers in institutional settings.

Leadership in Small Groups

Research on the dynamics of small groups in the 1950s provided key findings for the sociological study of power. This research was one basis for the development of the functionalist theory of society. Central to these studies was the investigation of authority, which can be defined as legitimate power. Informal groups were used, in order to understand the spontaneous process of role differentiation in groups. Formal organizations, whose leaders are officially designated personnel, do not show the grassroots process of leadership. A whole generation of sociology students read William Foote Whyte's classic, *Street Corner Society* (1943), which showed the informal leadership structure of a North Boston street gang in the Depression.

Parsons and Bales's studies (1955) involved experimental groups of paid students hired to work together in observation rooms to do cooperative problem solving. The experimenters carefully watched and documented the roles played by the subjects. These students had never met each other, and no leader was designated. The solution of the problems required that the group meet several times. The first leadership role to emerge was the "instrumental leader." This young man or woman was the person who organized and guided the group toward successful completion of the task. This leader tended to be an "ideas" person who took the task seriously, spurred the group members to concentrate on the task, and analyzed, criticized, and synthesized the ideas suggested by the other group members. The instrumental leader stirred ambivalent feelings in the group members, positive regard for the coordination and leadership but negative affect over the leader's criticalness and goal orientation. By the second group meeting, a second leader generally emerged in the group, the "expressive leader." This person had different personality traits from the instrumental leader, was more laid back, was oriented to feelings in contrast to the other leader who was thinking-oriented, and often was a joker. When the group life became tense around the problems of completing the task, the "expressive leader" had a capacity to bring some levity and tension release to the group atmosphere. Over time, a coalition often developed between the instrumental leader and the expressive leader, both evidencing respect for the contribution that the other made. Studying a wide range of informal groups, researchers found this same tendency for dual leadership. The idea of differentiated group functions and consequent leadership styles led to the many management consultant theories of group process, including LIFO Training (1978)[1] and other group self-study programs.

The much-heralded nuclear family of the 1950s, with its employed husband, homemaker wife, and two or three children, seemed to fit the model of the small group as revealed in the

Parsons and Bales experiments. Sure enough, the husband-father played the role of instrumental leader, being the breadwinner, task organizer, and disciplinarian. The wife-mother served as the expressive leader, dealing with the emotions of all family members and providing good-spirited nurture. Hence arose the model of the well-functioning family. The conflict tradition of sociology, as we will see below, criticized this viewpoint.

Pastoral care came under the influence of the same model. The church is a moral community, Parsons said (1964, 292–324), where the pastor is the instrumental leader, hammering on congregants' moral and spiritual obligations. A specialized ministry of pastoral care developed in the 1950s and 1960s, Parsons held, because pastors as instrumental leaders were necessarily prevented by their task responsibilities from also playing the expressive leader role. The pastoral counselor provided the emotional "space" for parishioners to explore their ambivalences and conflicts about the heavy moral demands of the religious life. The counselor, like a psychiatrist, exemplified high moral standards but relaxed the atmosphere enough for congregants experiencing what Parsons calls the "spiritual malaise" to come to grips with their feelings and achieve religious maturity.

The Functional Theory of Stratification

Parsons, in his later career, developed the idea of power as a quality of the society, not the individual (1969). Power is the capacity of a society to achieve its goals. There is a parallel between power in the political sphere and money in the economic sphere. Power is the trust that citizens have of their political leaders, based on the demonstrated or presumed responsibility of those leaders, manifested in a "blank check" given to the leaders to make decisions for the body politic. Like money, which through the credit system expands far beyond its base in real cash, power expands through the trust given to leaders to act for the common good without being "second-guessed" by the populace. When this trust dissolves, then the leaders cannot act freely, they avoid any significant initiatives, and the result is governmental paralysis. The loss of trust may, of course, be caused by the irresponsibility of the leaders who "play politics" rather than act as statesmen and -women.

The functional theory of stratification focuses on the differential rewards that lead to inequality. The key problem of a society, according to this theory, is motivating the most capable persons to assume the most important and responsible positions and to undergo the long training required. The high rewards for persons assuming those functionally most important positions is therefore justified. The key to social order in the functionalist view is making the channels of recruitment to high positions solely responsive to universalistic standards of achievement, not ascribed characteristics such as gender, race, economic class, or family origin. The ideal in this view of power and inequality is a thoroughgoing meritocracy. Davis and Moore (1945) and Parsons (1977) are quintessential liberals who stress individualistic civil rights. Individualistic feminists who aspire to career mobility unrestricted by their gender find the functionalist perspective on stratification quite congenial (cf. Fox-Genovese 1991). However, women *working* did not fit into Parsons's system because of the instrumental versus expressive leadership functions of the family!

The critique of the functionalist theory of stratification has several dimensions. Rewarding some position-occupants with high rewards because they fill the functionally most important positions, Tumin pointed out (1953), has the contrary effect on those who fill the lowly and less highly regarded jobs. If high salaries are strong incentives to some, low wages are a *disincentive* to those in lower-echelon positions. The possibility for sabotage of the system by disaffected workers points up the need for adequate rewards for *all* system members.

A similar criticism concerns the range or spread of inequality, which cannot be so great that the sense of a moral community is destroyed. Comparing the economy of the United States with that of Japan, we see the spread of worker salaries—the difference between the compensation of the top and bottom 10 percent of a firm's employees—to be much greater in the United States than in Japan. Such inequality stretches the lower-echelon workers' sense of legitimacy of the compensation system and creates the "equity" or "fairness" issue that some economists believe places the U.S. economy at an international competitive disadvantage (Thurow 1985).

Power viewed from the functionalist perspective stresses the conditions needed for a society to have effective collective decision-making and goal-attainment. The emphasis is upon achieving sufficient value-integration, integrity of leadership, and political "trust" of the electorate for government to work. This perspective cannot be stereotyped as a "conservative" ideology, for leftist thinkers like Jürgen Habermas (1975) of Germany express concern about the "legitimation crisis" facing Western democracies. Sociologists who were students of Talcott Parsons, most prominently Robert Bellah, express major alarm about the political implications of modern individualism. Bellah articulates this concern in terms of a social "broken covenant" (1975) and the loss of a collective sense of the "common good" (Bellah et al. 1985, 1991).

The Conflict Theory of Stratification

The conflict tradition became strong in American sociology in the late 1960s. This tradition goes back to Machiavelli and Hobbes and was articulated strongly by Marx and Engels. Randall Collins characterizes this perspective as "cynical realism."

Individuals' behavior is explained in terms of their self-interests in a material world of threat and violence. Social order is seen as being founded on organized coercion. There is an ideological realm of belief (religion, law), and an underlying world of struggles over power; ideas and morals are not prior to interaction but are socially created, and serve the interests of parties to the conflict. (1975, 57)

Marxian thought focuses attention on the society's "means of production" and its "relations of production." The means of production are the complex of technological developments for economic life: agriculture, manufacturing, commerce, communication, transportation. The relations of production are the social arrangements based on a particular means of production. Manufacturing involves basically two classes: entrepreneur-capitalists and factory workers, the oppressors and the oppressed. The "means of production" and the "relations of production" comprise the materialistic foundation of the society. Politics and the state, religion, and the legal system make up the ideological superstructure that expresses and gives legitimation to the class interests of the society's dominant classes. As the oppressed classes communicate, gain a sense of their true class interests, and organize, they become a revolutionary force able to overthrow the existing social order and institute a new society.

Marx and Engels, by stressing property ownership as the sole basis of power, oversimplified the picture of stratification dynamics in a modern society. Max Weber elaborated upon Marx and Engels's sociology and corrected some of its most glaring inadequacies. Weber's theory will be viewed here and especially in chapter 5, for he is a key figure in the sociology of religion.

Modern conflict sociology combines the Marxian-Weberian macrosociological tradition with microsociology, especially that of Erving Goffman and Harold Garfinkel. Goffman was an immensely perceptive observer of social rituals. The social order of stratification with its domination and subordination, its order and its conflict, is expressed in countless rituals of daily life. Goffman studied crofters (sheepherders) in the Shetland Islands, workers and supervisors in industry, bureaucratic offices, males and females interacting, and theatrical performers. Goffman viewed social life as the interaction of performers and audiences, persons alternating between these roles depending upon who was acting. A major social dynamic in Goffman's perspective is impression-management, where people control the situation in order to make the most favorable and desirable impression through the manipulation of environment, physical cues, and actions. We can use Goffman's mode of social analysis to understand how the power factor affects staff relationships in a health care institution.

The doctors' dining room at a large regional hospital can serve as an illustration of Goffmanesque sociological analysis. This was one of three dining rooms serving the hospital community. Two were for general staff and public use, but the doctors' dining room was for the exclusive use of the physicians. A doctor would occasionally eat with a chaplain or other staff member or the doctor's own spouse in one of the general-use dining rooms, but the norms prevented a physician from inviting any of these others to eat in the doctors' dining room. Until recently, the female physicians, a growing part of that hospital's medical staff, rarely ate in the doctors' dining room, a reaction perhaps to its "old boys" clubhouse ambience.

The segregation of eating space in the hospital seemed relatively unquestioned. People appeared to grant the doctors the right to eat in peace without having to interact with their patients' kinfolk or with the nurses, some of whom perceived them as "arrogant bastards." Professional conversation among physicians in a protected atmosphere allowed some relaxation of the norms of patient confidentiality. These were among the expressed and "accepted" reasons for the exclusive dining room. But other functions were served by the dining pattern that were not part of its official rationale. Segregation of eating space has high symbolic importance for maintenance of a hospital's power structure. Having a friendly exchange with a doctor in the cafeteria line, then experiencing the withdrawal of that physician to the elite "inner sanctum," reinforces for the other staff member the doctor's superior social rank in the institutional system. Segregated dining also provides insulation for the physicians from exposure to viewpoints in conflict with their official cognitive world regarding medicine and the healing arts. The doctors' dining room was thus a social mechanism for "reality-maintenance" of the doctors' worldview. It reinforced the medical establishment's selective perceptions of reality that can be linked to its economic, political, and gender interests. Social rituals reinforce a definition of the situation, positing a hierarchical relationship between social groups. The physician case is important, because it involves "approved" social inequality, not a blatant case like racial discrimination, such as white and "colored" restrooms.

Power issues insinuate themselves in organizations that maintain a strong "mission" of nondiscrimination. A large hospital asserted in its official statement of purpose that it offered care without consideration of economic status, creed, or other factors. Yet a special club existed for benefactors who contributed more than $10,000 to the hospital's charitable foundation. Unknown to the public and most staff, the hospital maintained a special locked room for exclusive use of the members of this club. This nicely appointed room had a telephone, a garden view, and a stocked refrigerator. Club members had use of this private room when a family member was hospitalized. On some patient lists generated by the hospital computer, a special code appeared next to the names of patients who belonged to the club families. No one overtly told hospital staff to be especially solicitous to these patrons, but the message seemed implied.

The contrast between the conflict and functionalist perspectives in sociology can be seen clearly when we look at their different understandings of the professions. The functionalists see the modern professions (medicine and law are the models) as the key to a well-functioning society. Because the value-system of the professional communities stresses achievement, universalism, affective-neutrality and collectivity-orientation, the professions are viewed as central to the solution of both the adaptive and integrative problems facing modern society. Talcott Parsons, in his laudatory attitude toward professions, maintains Durkheim's position that professional societies are the modern repository of social values.

In contrast, the conflict tradition understands professions as social groups mobilizing power for autonomy and enhanced social prestige. British sociologist Terence J. Johnson pioneered this approach in his *Professions and Power:*

> Professionalism becomes redefined as a peculiar type of occupational control rather than an expression of the inherent nature of particular occupations. A profession is not, then, an occupation, but a means of controlling an occupation. (1972, 45)

Professionalization, from this viewpoint, is the effort of an occupational group to increase its autonomy vis-à-vis other occupational groups, to create a monopoly over the provision of the given service through credentialing and licensing structures, and to use its improved public image as a "profession" to win greater economic compensation (Larson 1977; Collins 1979). Professions' autonomous control over access to membership has had significant gender implications (Witz 1992).

The conflict sociology perspective sheds a different light on a "model" professional relationship, which pastoral caregivers have admired and to some extent emulated, that of psychiatrist and patient in psychoanalysis. Power is defined in terms of asymmetrical relationships, the nonreciprocity of obligations of the role partners. The supervisor gives orders; the subordinate takes orders. Psychoanalysis is a classic case of an asymmetrical relationship. The analyst is under no obligation to reveal his or her vulnerability, feelings, or insecurities. (Several years of Freudian psychoanalysis in the 1960s gave me personal experience of the role asymmetry of analyst and analysand.) The therapeutic ritual establishes the analyst as undisturbed, above the fray, in control. Freud and his followers provided an elaborate rationale for the asymmetrical character of the analyst-patient relationship, including the necessity of creating a social structure that facilitates transference. Obviously, the analytic situation does this, but it is also a power trip for the analyst. The justification can be considered, in one important sense, ideological, the legitimation of a social structure that serves the interests of the power holders.

The Multidimensional Nature of Social Stratification

After Marx and Engels, Max Weber is the seminal thinker in the conflict tradition of sociology. His major contribution was to define the multidimensional character of stratification. He thereby avoided a pitfall of Marx and Engels's theory. As we will see, Weber's theory is very important for understanding where religious functionaries, and thus pastoral caregivers, stand in the stratification system. Weber rejects the notion of a unidimensional system of social status. Taking seriously Weber's multidimensional viewpoint causes us to realize that our usual sociological tendency to categorize people as upper class, middle class, working class, and lower class yields an oversimplified picture of the stratification order. There are at least three rankings, Weber held, comprising a stratification system. These are the economic, political, and "status" rankings. Wealth, power, and social prestige are the dimensions of these rankings. Stratification by wealth or occupation or property—all economic factors—generates classes. Stratification by power yields party hierarchies. Stratification by prestige yields status groups and, in societies highly ordered by social prestige, castes.

Weber's theory illuminates the dynamics of change in stratification. Individuals often occupy unequal positions on the three rankings of stratification. Thus African-American physicians possess what sociologists call *status inconsistency*, wherein their economic status (education, profession, and income) is high, but their "social" status (based on their ethnicity) is low. The old-time political boss also experienced status inconsistency, possessing extremely high power and often significant wealth, but having little education and low social prestige because of ethnicity (Irish-American, Italian-American) and his morally suspect involvement in political corruption. The *nouveaux riches*, persons who have gained new money but lack "social graces" and acceptance in upper-class social circles, are classic examples of status inconsistency. Status inconsistency is very disturbing to persons psychologically, for they do not "fit" in the accepted social order. These psychological stresses rooted in social structural reality cause these individuals to be agitators for social change, especially— where race is a factor—against racial discrimination. The leaders of nationalist movements in former European colonies typically were well-educated Africans and Asians whose occupational advancement and social acceptance were blocked because of their non-European ethnicity.

Religious leaders, whether Catholic priests and sisters, Protestant clergy, or Jewish rabbis, like college professors, experience status inconsistency. Their educational level is extremely high, their social status (at least within ecclesiastical circles) is very high, yet their income is low. This fact has often made clergy feel somehow "above" class and caste. This attitude is quite erroneous because religious communities are status groups, and social prestige has other roots besides economic assets. In the traditional religion of tribal societies, there is no difference between a person's religious position and his or her worldly position. Prosperity, health, and victory in war reflected the blessing of the gods. The transcendental religions (Christianity, Islam, and Confucianism) changed this. They posit the existence of two realms, the worldly and the eternal or transcendent. Worldly success is no longer co-equal with religious status. The orgiastic religious rituals of the tribal societies are replaced by interiority, mysticism, and emotional and physical control. Extensive knowledge of sacred scripture becomes the source of prestige and power within the religious community. Worldly affluence is perceived as an obstacle to religious communion. In religious circles, the negotiation of status by no means ceases; only the resources used to assert one's position are redefined.

Gender and Stratification

The conflict sociology approach to pastoral care generates heightened consciousness of the "power factor" in all social relationships. This is especially true in the field of gender relations. This consciousness was lacking in the functionalist perspective that viewed the nuclear family with its "instrumental leader" husband and "expressive leader" wife as the model. There was a presumption of equal power of the two partners based on their spheres of influence. This basic model undergirded early family systems therapy. The stress was on equilibrium and harmony (Boss and Thorne 1989).

Denied in this model was women's experience. Feminist sociologists observed that the normal family model of equal power and equilibrium was an ideology. Jessie Bernard (1972), for example, coined the apt phrase, the "His and Hers" marriage. The man and woman have engaged in the same activities, have been involved in the same conversations, have shared the same bed, are parents of the same children, but have radically different perceptions of their marriage. Typically, the man believes things are good and the woman believes they are bad.

Sociologists point out that the "model," the nuclear family of employed husband, full-time homemaker wife, and their children, represents only a small number of contemporary families. A major crisis faces women who work and have children. Studies show that husbands of full-time employed wives do little more housework and childcare than husbands whose wives are full-time homemakers. The result is women's anger over the power inequality between men and women.

Erving Goffman sees the politics of gender as crucial in the stratification system. "Gender, not religion, is the opiate of the masses" (1987, 63). Marx and Engels said religion created false consciousness in the masses, defusing their hostility to the existing class structure by creating the hope of an eternal promised land. Goffman sees gender relations between men and women as having the same effect. Because men operate from a consciousness of power superiority in relationship to women, they get an ego boost that defuses the frustration over their powerlessness in the larger structures of the economy.

Pastoral care is criticized for its failure to take women's experience seriously. Moessner and Glaz give this case:

June, a mother for the first time, had had a harrowing delivery: she nearly died in childbirth. Exhausted and frightened, she lay awake in her hospital bed unable to close her eyes. She was glad that the birthing process was finished, but the baby, she felt, had nearly killed her. When her pastor arrived, five hours had passed since the ordeal.

She could not bring herself to describe her feelings: the pastor, aware that she had been near death, did not inquire. Instead, after introductory talk, the pastor repeated how grateful to God she should be for the wonderful new life that had been entrusted to her. June felt even worse after the visit because one major part of her experience had not been acknowledged: the baby as threat to her own life.

June did, however, have two more children. Although she would not tell her husband the reason, she asked him to keep the minister away from her during her hospital stay at each birth. These two births were uncomplicated; June felt much better in her mothering of each. Because the youngest child seemed to do as well as her first child did poorly, June inferred that the minister's absence was far more helpful than his presence. (1991, 1)

This case illustrates how an idealized pastoral image of the family and of gender roles detracts from serious attention to the real feelings and actual experience of careseekers.

Gender issues of power become mixed with other issues in pastoral care. Helen, a fifty-year-old teacher and mother of three children, sought counseling with a female secular counselor. She said she was depressed and angry. Helen is the wife of a church pastor. She rejected pastoral counseling as an option because she believed "pastors would immediately side with John," her husband.

Helen told her counselor that John had been in his current position for more than ten years and had a very informal and friendly relationship with members of the suburban congregation, especially the women. She reported that a respected psychologist had told her husband that he had "a positive mother image" and that was why he could relate well to women. A considerable amount of his counseling was with "needy women," she said, who appreciated the way John made them feel important. Each day Helen saw her husband go off to work excited about the possibilities of the day, but she suspected not a little of that excitement came from the chance to "flirt with" the female members of the church staff and counsel with women—young and older—who gave his masculinity a big boost, perceiving him as a different kind of male: the sensitive, nonsexist, somewhat vulnerable counselor. Despite her significant Christian education role in the congregation, Helen reported that John's female "entourage" was thrilled to see him but paid no attention to her. She felt "invisible." Helen reported that John admitted to infatuation, "some little feelings," toward several of the women. He explained these feelings as natural for men to have and of no consequence.

After several sessions, the counselor suggested that it might be helpful to bring John into the sessions. John related easily to the counselor, said that he had "normal" interaction with the female parishioners and his counselees, and denied ever seeking or engaging in an illicit relationship. Helen felt again that this was a triangle with the counselor and her husband forming a liaison against her, "the jealous wife." After a few sessions with John, the counselor suggested that he was no longer needed in the sessions and that the focus should be on why Helen constantly felt so threatened. Helen decided these individual sessions were unfruitful and soon terminated the counseling.

Helen began attending pastoral care workshops. A religious perspective on counseling and healing was presented. Helen and John read books together setting forth a religious perspective on typical compulsions of men and women. John realized that his behavior, although not immoral from a secular point of view, was at variance with a standard of "purity." He came to admit that he was getting a "sexual gain" from his counseling work. Helen could feel her anger had been legitimate and that she was not "paranoid" or crazy. John became able to risk damaging his image as the kind, understanding pastor by learning to communicate in a clearer and more direct way with women.

This case points up the "power factor" in gender issues, the taken-for-granted character of gender interaction that gives a sense of power to men and makes women feel powerless. The counselor in this case, although female, was unable to cut through the other issues to the power dimension. Counseling that focuses on intrapsychic dynamics fails to take account of the larger cultural context that fuels the careseeker's anger and depression.

Race, Stratification, and Pastoral Care

The complexities of stratification become evident in modern America and Europe when we observe how racial identity crosscuts other identities. As Weber observed, socioeconomic status based on education, income, and occupational ranking is a separate ranking from prestige. Ethnic stratification ranks status groups. Black-white relations is a status group problem. The complexity of race and other identities was revealed in the reaction of African-American women to the Clarence Thomas/Anita Hill hearings on sexual harassment. Black women were deeply divided over the dilemma of protecting a black man from attack by whites and identifying with a woman (black or otherwise) over harassment by males.

Noted black sociologist and University of Chicago professor William J. Wilson, in *The Truly Disadvantaged* (1987), advances an important thesis on America's urban situation. Using massive data, Wilson challenges Reagan-era assumptions about welfare policy. He then puts forth a striking observation about leadership in the inner cities. The civil rights gains of the 1960s and 1970s broke down the suburban restrictions on housing for upper-income blacks, the African-American leadership class. Previously, housing discrimination had forced these ethnic group members to live in the inner cities, and they provided leadership and social control in those neighborhoods. The opening up of the suburbs to black homeownership meant the loss of those leaders in the inner city. Wilson holds that structural problems in the economy (such as the lack of employment removing incentive for high school completion) are the primary cause of the increase of inner-city drug use, violent crime, and other urban problems; however, he believes the leadership exodus is an important secondary cause. Pastoral care confronts this problem in the ambivalence of middle-class African-American men and women who value the opportunity to join the American mainstream but feel guilt about deserting their ethnic brothers and sisters.

Another problem pastoral care faces is the ethnic prejudice of white Protestant and Catholic careseekers, many of whom are "religious" people. Pastoral caregivers have not consistently challenged the overt and subtle prejudice met in careseekers on grounds that this alienates the person and weakens the possibility of working long-term with that individual. We will look specifically at this issue in the chapter on the sociology of religion.

Work, Alienation, and Pastoral Care

The larger social context of economy, polity, and culture impacts the pastoral care process both as a contributing cause of careseekers' problems and as an opportunity for meaningful involvement for change.

Marilyn was an African-American member of a smaller urban congregation. In her late thirties, she was a single parent raising two children, a teenage girl and a boy aged twelve. She and her children lived in a small but comfortable single-family home in an all-black neighborhood. One of the "lucky" ones in her neighborhood who had a job, she was employed as an assembly-line worker in a large industrial plant. The company had a policy of staffing its factories with two shifts of workers, each working eight hours daily under conditions of normal demand but this could increase to as many as twelve hours a day when demand was high. The firm's rationale for expanding the hours of the existing work force rather than hiring new workers for a third eight-hour shift was it could not afford to pay the generous benefit package for additional workers.

Marilyn worked the evening shift, leaving home in the afternoon and returning in the wee small hours. Her work on the assembly line was very physically demanding. At a previous time, she had suffered a severe back strain. Under normal work hours, her back problem did not flare up. But at the time under consideration here, the work force was on twelve-hour shifts six days a week because of heavy demand. Overwork had exacerbated her back injury; her life was a relentless alternation of work and painful sleep. Marilyn succeeded in avoiding drug use or excessive alcohol consumption, which mushroomed at this time among her coworkers. She was determined to keep working and to keep her job, upon which her family's economic security depended.

Marilyn rarely made it to church worship at this time. Her pastor visited her in her home from time to time. She was unreachable by phone, which she unplugged because she slept during the day. Marilyn asked for basic spiritual support from her pastor. "Pray for me that I can *survive!*" She was concerned also about her children, whom she praised for managing "pretty well" on their own most of the time.

Marilyn's case points up the issue of structural evil and powerlessness. Pastoral care for Marilyn could not ask her to be adjusted to the "system." Only some sense of empowerment that gave this conscientious worker, *together with others,* a voice in changing the inhumane structures could be the ultimate goal of her pastoral care. Marilyn felt desperation, but part of that desperation arose from her atomization. She had little sense of social bond with other workers, who could together feel some power in influencing the conditions of their common employment. True, she belonged to one of the most powerful labor unions in the United States. The material rewards—pay and benefits—negotiated by the union leaders were extraordinary, and during the period of overtime and often doubletime pay, she and her co-workers were bringing home the biggest paychecks they had ever earned. These rewards, however, seemed to deepen the alienation of the workers, who perhaps had the Faustian sense of selling their souls to the devil. Pastoral care in Marilyn's case was a stopgap thing, getting her through from one day to the next. Some meaningful involvement in collective social change, even if only in a small group, could reduce her sense of powerlessness.

Mediating Structures and Empowerment

Howard Clinebell succinctly articulates the political dimension of care and counseling:

> Working to change the wider systems that diminish people's growth often is essential to sustain growth within them and their close relationships. Rather than adjusting people to growth-crippling institutions, constructive counseling and therapy seek to *empower* people to work with others to change the institutional and societal roots of individual problems. (1981, 18)

Clinebell states this imperative in terms of self-psychology and the benefits for sustained personal growth. From a religious point of view, persons bear the responsibility for shaping a humane social order. However one looks at empowerment, the integral link of individual and society is clear.

Social theorists from Alexis de Tocqueville, Durkheim, and Weber forward have asserted the necessity for a level of social organization between individuals' primary groups of family and work group and the societywide structures of national government, economy, and communication. The lack of such *mediating structures* creates what political scientists of the fifties and sixties termed "the mass society" (Kornhauser 1959). Mediating structures are organized neighborhoods, religious organizations, voluntary associations, local government, ethnic groupings, and organized social movements. Participation in such structures helps overcome the alienation experienced in modern society by mediating between the private and public spheres. As Berger and Neuhaus observe,

> Such [mediating structures] have a private face, giving private life a measure of stability, and they have a public face, transferring meaning and value to the megastructures. (1977, 3)

Empowerment in pastoral care involves careseekers discovering the alternatives to being a victim. Small, militant minorities have enormous power, when organized and channeled, to influence modern political life.

Many examples exist of concerned citizens banding together to exert political influence over a situation they deem evil. Employees of the United States National Forest Service have a major center in Eugene, Oregon, headquarters of the massive Willamette National Forest of Oregon. The environmental consciousness of many Forest Service workers caused them to have grave moral reservations about federal national forest policies formulated by the Reagan and Bush administrations. These policies made a mockery of the established "sustained yield" principle of timber cutting and wreaked havoc on the Western mountainous environment. Jeff DeBonis, a concerned and articulate Forest Service employee, deeming it futile for atomized individual personnel scattered in different departments and offices to decry the policies privately, organized a protest group, the Association of Forest Service Employees for Environmental Ethics. This group became a nucleus for public action by a group of trained persons who knew the exact dimensions of the problem. This organization has grown and now exerts significant influence at both the regional and national levels.

Pastoral care assists careseekers in finding a sense of divine vocation and in facilitating their empowerment through participation in mediating structures to have a meaningful impact on their society and its larger structures.

Conclusion

The sociological approach to pastoral care points up the reality of power in social relationships. The larger structures of power and inequality intrude upon pastoral care. Psychology and family systems therapy frequently ignore the power dynamics in the careseeker's situation. The major stratification variables of race, class, gender, and age crosscut the social context of care in sometimes complicated ways. The existing power structure is reinforced by social rituals whereby persons seek to control the definition of the situation. Pastoral care involves exploring alternative definitions of the situation, based on egalitarian rather than hierarchical power models, and empowering careseekers to change societal structures.

5. The Sociology of Religion and Pastoral Care

This chapter represents an effort to reunite what became severed in pastoral care: the sociology of religion and the psychology of religion. Anton Boisen, the pioneer of modern pastoral care who was both a sociologist and psychologist, held these two perspectives in integral connection (see, for example, Boisen 1955). Boisen's followers, however, concentrated almost solely on the psychology of religion and failed to maintain a vital link with the sociology of religion as a source of guidance for pastoral care.

A word about the psychology of religion first. As developed by such pastoral caregivers as Wayne E. Oates (1973) and Orlo Strunk, Jr. (1965), it focuses on the process of religious development toward what they call "healthy religion" or "mature religion." Oates writes:

> The psychologist of religion takes a closer look at the root and nourishment of the plant [religion] and does not just admire the beauty of the flower and enjoy the fruit. The practical, optimal result of this closer and more critical look is to provide basic data for reproducing healthy religion in persons and for offsetting the blights and diseases that assail religious growth. At this point, psychology of religion and pastoral care join forces, the first becoming the conceptual basis for adequate care and cure of souls. (1973, 43)

Thus Oates and Strunk challenge pastoral caregivers to maintain a critical attitude toward the religion of their careseekers. Their healthy religion is what this book talks about as religious definitions of the situation found adequate by careseekers to withstand the tests of life crises.

The sociology of religion provides a vital perspective for understanding careseekers' growth toward healthy religion. This subfield of sociology studies the religious sector of the society and its relationship to the other institutional sectors including the economy, the political order, and the family system. It investigates the sources and consequences of religious belief and behavior and the dynamics of religious organization and community. Since religious definitions of situations have their anchorage in religious communities, the cultural and organizational dynamics of these communities exert a formative influence upon the shape of those definitions. Sociologists of religion offer pastoral caregivers a clearer picture of the religious options available to the modern careseeker and the implications of different choices.

This chapter highlights two central concepts in the sociology of religion, secularization and alienation. The first of these concepts was introduced in chapter 2 on the sociology of knowledge. Here we look at secularization as it impacts the dynamics of religious organizations.

Alienation is the process whereby religious perspectives are taken captive by cultural forces and lose their transcendent and critical edge. Sociologists distinguish alienating and de-alienating religion, the former being culturally captive and the latter, prophetic and liberating.[1] Alienating religion provides ideological justification for social inequality, whether in the form of economic hierarchy, political oppression, patriarchal structures, or ethnic stratification. The concepts of alienating and de-alienating religion are the sociological equivalents of the psychological concepts, unhealthy and healthy religion, and thus are useful in our effort to integrate the sociology and psychology of religion as employed by pastoral caregivers.

To introduce the sociology of religion, this chapter begins with a case study of pastoral care within a local church, showing how the religious culture of the congregation affects the outcome of the pastoral care process. Next the functionalist and conflict traditions of the sociology of religion are compared. It is argued that much present-day pastoral care operates from the functionalist viewpoint and implicitly encourages alienating religion. Then, using the conflict perspective, we create a model of the dynamics of religious communities that shows how secularization, alienation, and de-alienation interact. Next a corollary model of theological responses to the modern situation is presented. Three resultant types of such theology are identified, types that distinguish styles of pastoral care. One of these types of theology, the inductive, orients the sociological approach to pastoral care offered in this book. Finally, we draw together the different strands of analysis from the sociology of religion to suggest how this perspective helps strengthen pastoral care and how pastoral caregivers can best encourage healthy religion—the de-alienated form—in careseekers.

Pastoral Care and
Congregational Life

The sociology of religion investigates how the dominant culture of a society affects the culture of its religious communities. Though their organizational ties to those communities vary, pastoral caregivers operate within these communities' general boundaries, and their cultures influence the outcome of the pastoral care process. So we have a two-step process, the dominant societal ethos shaping the religious communities' cultures and those cultures affecting the work of pastoral care. The effect of the larger societal culture and the smaller congregational culture on pastoral care is illustrated in the following case.

Robert and Carole, a married couple in their thirties, belong to a Protestant congregation whose culture reflects the American ethos of individualism. Central to that culture are the norms of personal privacy and individual responsibility. Both Carole and Robert are active church members, involved in the Christian education program and in church boards. Members of the congregation have been aware for some time of their stormy marriage. Then suddenly the couple separate. Robert moves out of the house, leaving Carole and their four children to carry on. Carole belongs to an old church family, and she has the full sympathy of most congregation members in regard to the marriage crisis. Robert is judged the culpable partner, for he walked out on his wife. Robert comes to church a few times following the breakup but receives a very negative reception and then is no longer seen. Carole and the children continue to come to church. She maintains some of her usual roles, but then her participation, as well as that of the children, becomes infrequent.

Two pastors of the church are involved in counseling with Robert and Carole. Through their confidential pastoral relationship with the couple, they have learned the precipitating cause of the breakup is Carole's extramarital affair. This "secret" is unknown to the members of the congregation. The pastors face a dilemma. They believe that unless the church members know the facts of the situation, they cannot give support to the pastors' efforts to achieve the couple's reconciliation. Without this knowledge, the congregation will maintain an unrealistically positive image of Carole and negative image of Robert. However, they understand the norms governing the congregation stress personal privacy and proscribe "washing dirty linen in public." They have little power to compel Carole to make an honest disclosure of her illicit relationship, something she refuses to do voluntarily. Moreover, the pastors realize the church members understand the success or failure of marriages in terms of the individual responsibility of the partners. The congregation thus feels little responsibility for calling partners to account as a step toward "saving" troubled relationships. In a congregation with a different culture, where the right of the community to know personal facts about the members outweighs the right of individual privacy, the pastors could confront Carole with the choice of either disclosing her affair to the congregation or having them do so. What the outcome of Robert and Carole's crisis would have been had the congregation participated in the pastoral care process, the pastors do not know. However, under the constraints of the individualistic culture, the pastors feel there is little they can do beyond their private counsel.

This case illustrates the cultural context in which much American pastoral care occurs. Several critiques of contemporary pastoral care, as we saw in chapter 1, focus on the character of religious organizations. Especially emphasized is the individualistic ethos of many churches, a reflection of the value system of the larger society. This ethos is manifested in Robert and Carole's congregation, a middle-class white Protestant church. Noteworthy today is that the African-American congregation is held up as an exemplary context of pastoral care. Archie Smith, Jr. (1982) launches his critique, *The Relational Self*, from the vantage point of the black church. More recently, Don Browning (1992) has used a pentecostal African-American congregation as a model of pastoral care. Both books assert that the individualistic community lacks the strong social bonds that support effective Christian pastoral care.

The Functionalist Perspective on Religion

The two traditions in sociology surveyed in the last chapter regarding their understanding of power and stratification have significantly different attitudes toward religion. In this section, we will review the sociology of religion as it is understood by the functionalists. The next section covers the conflict theorists' argument.

The functionalist viewpoint stresses the social benefit of religion for people's motivation to perform their expected social roles despite existential uncertainty. Bronislaw Malinowski (1954) made this functionalist argument when he reported on the fishing practices of the Trobriand islanders. Lagoon fishing in the coral atoll islands had no directly related religious or magical ceremonies. Open-sea fishing, however, was steeped in religion, every phase of which was carefully governed by ritual. The significant difference between the two modes of fishing, Malinowski observed, was the predictability and safety of lagoon fishing compared with the unpredictability and high danger of open-sea fishing. Religion relates human beings to the realm of mystery and uncertainty and provides assurances that overcome fear.

The functionalist perspective received its classic articulation in the lifetime preoccupation of the French sociologist Émile Durkheim. He asked, what is the "social glue" that holds modern societies together and provides motivational incentive for modern people to work productively within an increasingly complex division of labor and to fulfill their civic responsibilities? Durkheim (1915) asserted that religion in premodern societies had the function of integrating the society and providing a supernatural context for social participation. But in modern societies, Durkheim held, religion ceases to fulfill that function; being contrary to modern science, religion is implausible for an increasingly larger segment of the population. Thus he believed a secular equivalent of religion is required to provide the moral underpinning of the modern society. Durkheim placed his hope in occupational and professional associations, the modern equivalent of the medieval guilds, as "schools" for inculcating in their members the proper social attitudes required of modern economies and societies.

The functionalists, most prominently the late Talcott Parsons, have stressed the *latent* function of religion. That is, whatever its manifest or expressed purpose of relating people to the divine order, the important sociological consideration is its unrecognized but significant benefit for societal integration.

> Religion might not be true, but, for this functionalist school, it was certainly good—in fact it was indispensable. It established a focus for community loyalty; provided occasions for the expression of group cohesion; it supplied a basis for social control; it legitimated group activities, polities, and policies; it interpreted the cosmos; and it facilitated, and also regulated, the expression of appropriate emotion. (Wilson 1982, 169)

Parsons was careful not to question the truth claims of religions, asserting that sociology can deal only with the truth of empirical matters and that the ultimate basis of religion is nonempirical. However, Parsons was very critical of any religious fundamentalisms that make religion a divisive force in the society. His desired religion was eminently tolerant and supportive of the "societal community," what Robert Bellah (1970, 168–89) terms a "civil religion." Parsons, like his intellectual father Durkheim, emphasized the modern societal importance of secular professional associations for shoring up the moral community, fulfilling the same function religion had at an earlier time.

The functionalist argument for religion is deeply institutionalized in American society. This viewpoint says that religion, so long as it is tolerant, subdued, and private, is "good" for people. Critics call this viewpoint "belief in belief." The truth claims of the religious assertions do not matter; the key is that people believe something. The functionalist viewpoint was the basis for a much-quoted remark by Dwight Eisenhower in which he extolled the virtue of religious belief as a foundation for the American political system, religious belief "whatever it is." (Leinberger and Tucker 1991, 146) Opposed to overt conflict in the society, functionalists stress that religious belief should be a private matter. They deem illegitimate any effort by religious people to argue for their worldview as "public truth."

The functionalist viewpoint often provides the institutional justification for departments of pastoral care in hospitals and other care facilities. Because of the correlation between religious faith and physical and emotional health, institutional administrators deem it wise to deploy chaplains and other pastoral workers whose services to patients and their families may result in shorter hospitalizations and in reduced patient demand for unnecessary nursing care. The problem with the use of this functionalist rationale to legitimate pastoral care is not, of course, related to the personal benefits of religious faith for persons' mental and physical health. Rather it relates to the way religion is not treated as a value in its own right but is subordinated to other institutional values. It is thus suspect when those other goals are not achieved. We see this in the way the functionalist viewpoint undergirds the attitude of other staff toward hospital chaplains. On at least two occasions as a chaplain, I experienced a situation in which a patient's condition significantly worsened during or immediately following my visit. In one case, the heart monitor of a patient who was talking with me about major emotional and spiritual issues revealed marked irregularity to staff at the nursing station. In the other case, a patient had a cardiac arrest a few minutes after a significant pastoral conversation. In both cases, my role was challenged—humorously but with some seriousness—"You're supposed to be making people well— and see what happens!" Similarly, because religion is supposed to yield harmonious relationships and calm troubled waters, chaplains are expected to be good-spirited at all times. Unit staff members are often shocked when the chaplain shows anger about something.

The functionalist tradition of the sociology of religion, in short, stresses how religion benefits the society by generating in its members the motivation to play needed roles and by instilling commitment to the social order. To use an image from mechanics, religion represents a centripetal force drawing human beings toward the societal center and counteracts the centrifugal forces of human selfishness, conflict, fear, and meaninglessness.

The Conflict Tradition of
The Sociology of Religion

The conflict perspective focuses attention upon how religious ideologies express and legitimate the economic, political, and status interests of social groups. As we saw in the last chapter, this tradition has roots in Hobbes and Machiavelli, was given its modern shape by Karl Marx and Friedrich Engels, and was further developed by Max Weber. Liberation theology is informed by this tradition of sociology.

The key idea in the Marxian tradition of sociology is alienation. "Alienation may be described as a condition in which men are dominated by forces of their own creation, which confront them as alien powers" (Coser 1971, 50). Religions, political systems, and economic systems are human constructions, but they take on a superhuman reality, a transcendent character, that makes their object— God or the gods, monarchy and aristocracy, capitalism—appear essential, immutable, and eternal.

In chapter 4, we looked at Marx and Engels's theory of social change as the dynamic tension between three elements: the society's means of production, its relations of production, and its ideological superstructure. The ideological superstructure—religion, government, morality, "culture"—expresses the power interests of the competing classes. The dominant ideology of the society represents the socioeconomic interests of the ruling class. Although exploited classes have the potential to express their economic interests in religious and political ideology, the social system of power relationships works against their doing so. The lower classes are especially subject to *false consciousness*, the absorption of the dominant religious, political, and economic worldview that "explains" their subordinate position. Marx and Engels are famous for their assertion that religion is the opiate of the people. They considered otherworldly religion, promising "pie in the sky by and by," to be a mechanism that narcotized the masses against consciousness of their present oppression. Class consciousness arises as oppressed people develop organization and realize their true class interests.[2]

Gerhard Lenski (1966, 1974) gives a good example of the conflict sociological view of religion in his analysis of social stratification in agrarian societies. Like Marx and Engels, Lenski sees advances in technology as the key to stratification. In the simplest societies, the hunting and gathering societies exemplified by the Kalahari Bushmen skillfully depicted in the popular film *The Gods Must Be Crazy*, little social inequality exists between families. Being nomadic and with all adults engaged in virtually full-time food production, hunting and gathering societies have little division of labor or unequal control of property. Horticultural societies, whose economy involves cultivation of small gardens, have greater division of labor but still relatively little social inequality.

The major leap to a stratified social order came historically in the agrarian societies, the empires of Egypt, Mesopotamia, Rome, China, and feudal Europe. The technological development responsible for these hierarchical societies was the agricultural revolution that, for the first time, created the possibility of a food surplus. The invention of the plow led to vastly increased soil productivity, made possible the use of oxen and other animals in the cultivation of crops, and caused the development of grain crops that could be transported and stored in granaries. The food surplus generated a larger division of labor, the rural peasantry producing food for an urban elite of king, priests, and artisans.

Religion provided an ideological justification for the forced removal of the food surplus from the agricultural worker's control through heavy taxation. The religious system defined all the land as belonging to the gods and designated the king as the gods' earthly agent. Hence the peasantry or serfs "owed" a large portion of their food production to the king and the priestly establishment as a "tithe." The new urban aristocracy sponsored the rise of the various artisan crafts (metalwork, stonework, armor making, writing) whose workers produced the material magnificence of the royal houses.

Religious legitimation of social inequality is not confined to historic agrarian societies. Modern industrialized societies also utilize religion in this way. A major instance was the religious ideological support for the system of racial apartheid in South Africa. As H. Richard Niebuhr showed in *The Social Sources of Denominationalism* (1929), economic class interests find strong expression in the denominational divisions of the body of Christ and their theological justification.

The conflict tradition of sociology focuses on the tendency of religious belief systems to disguise the economic and political interests of castes, classes, and genders behind a facade of objectivity. Religion is alienating when it "mystifies" the social construction of economic and political institutions. That is, when we say that a particular social order is ordained by God or the gods, we lose awareness of the fact that the social order is a human social product. Alienating religion is a form of "false consciousness," militating against people's sense of responsibility for establishing a just social order. A major thrust of the conflict tradition's sociology of religion is to expose the social interests behind religious ideologies and organizations.

Surveys conducted by sociologists of religion of the contemporary American population show a positive correlation between religious belief and support for social inequality. A number of studies, including a large University of California study in the late 1960s (Stark and Glock 1968) funded by a major grant from the Anti-Defamation League of B'nai B'rith, a leading Jewish organization, have found statistically significant higher rates of racial prejudice, anti-Semitism, anti-Catholicism (among Protestants), social and political conservatism, and psychological authoritarianism among respondents high on religious orthodoxy and level of church participation. Social prejudice as expressed in these attitudes when justified by religion constitutes what this book calls alienating religion.

Pastoral caregivers confront a difficult problem over the issue of alienating religion. They realize that careseekers need support communities to progress in their emotional and spiritual growth. As we saw in chapter 2, careseekers' religious definitions of the situation are likely to wither and die without involvement in a strong plausibility structure. If the caregiver is an institutional chaplain, she or he may want to recommend that a careseeker engaged in a spiritual quest become connected with a congregation or other spiritual community. However, there may be a dilemma here over the appropriate community for this referral. The local religious communities strongest in terms of spiritual support and small group networks often (but not always, of course) have cultural orientations that the chaplain may feel are contrary to the gospel: patriarchy, opposition to racial and economic justice, militarism, and disregard of the environment. The pastoral caregiver does not want to make careseeker referrals to communities that inculcate alienating religion.

The problem is exemplified in the case of a woman in her early thirties who was involved in the drug culture and permissive society of a large western city. Like the prodigal son, she "came to herself," sought spiritual counsel, and was directed to a nondenominational church oriented to young men and women coming out of addiction and the counterculture. For the first few months, she found the heavily structured legalistic life of this congregation very satisfying. It allowed her to find stability in her life for the first time in years. However, as her existence settled down and she found her bearings, she was increasingly angered by the patriarchal structure of the church. Women were definitely second class citizens, kept in a subordinate role by strong teaching and sanctions. Despite her appreciation of the church for its contribution to her recovery, she wondered how much longer she could stand being involved. The dilemma of pastoral referrals illustrated in this case will be examined further later in this chapter.

To sum up, two contrasting images of religion emerge in the sociology of religion, one—the functionalist—portraying religion or its equivalent as a necessary source of societal integration and social cooperation, the other—the conflict tradition—depicting religion as an instrument of oppression and alienation. Are the two images totally incompatible or do we have an opportunity to achieve some synthesis as a sociological perspective for pastoral care? In the next section, through the presentation of a model of the dynamics of religious communities, we will see how such a synthesis is possible. This model depends heavily on the bridging insights of Max Weber, a central figure in the sociology of religion, whose perspective is claimed by both the functionalists and the conflict theorists.

The Dynamics of Religious Communities

Peter Berger, in his major book on the sociology of religion, *The Sacred Canopy* (1967), speaks about the *alienating* and *de-alienating* functions of religion vis-à-vis the dominant social and political order. As stated above, religion is alienating when it "mystifies" the social construction of economic and political institutions. It is de-alienating when, as in prophetic Israel, it causes human institutions to be understood as existing under the radical transcendence of God. Berger's understanding that religion could be either alienating or de-alienating has its roots in Max Weber's revision of Marx and Engels's theory of religion. Weber in his studies of the religions of India, China, ancient Judaism, and Protestant Christianity identified world-rejecting and world-transforming religious movements that expressed a primary theological vision. Such movements were led by charismatic leaders absorbed in religious experiences that radically upset the existing religious and social order. The original vision of such charismatic leaders and their early followers constitutes what Berger and others call de-alienating religion.

Weber's multifaceted theory concerning the dynamics of religion in ancient and modern societies has inspired many scholars to develop and expand particular Weberian insights. Putting Weber's original conceptions and the newer elaborations together, we can create a model of the dynamics of religious communities. This model indicates the stages of tension between religious movements and the "worldly" social order as such movements develop over time. These stages are represented in figure 5-1.

As we examine this model, the reader is alerted to the constant intersection of the sociology and psychology of religion. Psychological needs of a religious character generate corporate religious activity and movements. The resulting religious communities change over time, causing a reduction in satisfaction of the original psychological needs. Tension rises, generating new religious behaviors and new communities. And on it goes. Pastoral care responds to both the psychological needs expressed in religious belief and activity and to the religious communities that sometimes satisfy but at other times frustrate these needs.

Charismatic Origins

Religious movements have their origin, Weber asserted, in the charismatic band, a group made up of a visionary leader and that individual's followers. For Weber, charisma is that special power of some leaders that followers perceive derives from a supernatural or divine source. Founders of religions are charismatic leaders who oppose worldly concerns in favor of transcendent objects and goals, which take the form either of world-rejection or world-transformation. Weber had Jesus and his disciples in mind as one of his major cases of charismatic authority. In its early stage, the charismatic organization of leader and followers strongly opposes the present existing world.

Visionary religious experiences are central to the existence of the charismatic band. Peter Berger, following Mircea Eliade, speaks of these dramatic visionary experiences as hierophanies, manifestations of the sacred.

> Any hierophany is experienced as the breaking-in of an other reality into the reality of ordinary human life. . . . the hierophany carries within itself its own warrant of certainty. That is, any individual standing within this experience is compelled by

it to exclaim, "Yes, yes, this is truth—and it could be no other."
Every hierophany is like thunder, and the human beings who
hear it must feel that this thunder blots out every other sound
in the universe. (1979, 88–89)

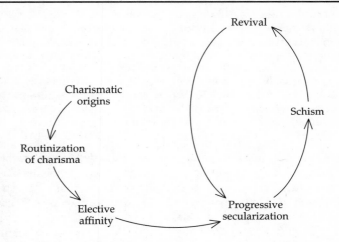

FIG. 5-1. A model of the dynamics of religious communities

Berger considers Jesus' disciples' experience of Calvary, Easter,
and Pentecost and the Muslim experience of the Night of Qadr as
revelatory hierophanies of this world-shattering type.

The charismatic origin of a religious movement, based in hierophanic experiences, can be characterized as de-alienating religion. Of course, the witnesses describe hierophanies in the
cognitive modes and language systems of their own culture, but
the visionary experience dissolves their social differences and
shifts their attention away from the pursuit of economic and social
interests to another realm of reality.

The Routinization of Charisma

The charismatic movement undergoes significant change with
the passage of time. As time passes, some degree of accommodation is made with the "world." Weber calls this accommodation

the routinization of charisma. He describes the social imperatives necessitating this accommodation in the following way:

> In its pure form charismatic authority has a character specifically foreign to everyday routine structures. The social relationships directly involved are strictly personal, based on the validity and practice of charismatic personal qualities. If this is not to remain a purely transitory phenomenon, but to take on the character of a permanent relationship forming a stable community of disciples or a band of followers or a party organization or any sort of political or hierocratic organization, it is necessary for the character of charismatic authority to become radically changed. Indeed, in its pure form charismatic authority may be said to exist only in the process of originating. It cannot remain stable, but becomes either traditionalized or rationalized, or a combination of both. (Weber 1947b, 363–64)

Thus the movement's stability and survival depend upon the solution of mundane economic, political, and social problems that were given little attention in the initial charismatic phase. An economic system develops that provides financial resources. A political structure emerges, especially to solve the problem of leadership succession posed by the death of the charismatic leader. In short, the tension between the movement and the social environment diminishes. The radical otherworldliness of the early movement changes to greater preoccupation with this-worldly interests. At the psychological level, this phase of "routinization of charisma" is characterized by the cooling down of emotional fervor in the movement's followers.

Elective Affinity

The charismatic leader and followers in the initial otherworldly stage of a religious movement are not oriented to economic or other social interests. But with the routinization of charisma, as the movement adapts to worldly existence, a process of *elective affinity* happens whereby followers of the religious movement "elect" certain ideas of the charismatic religious vision that fit their worldly interests, and other persons in the larger society who have those social interests find these ideas appealing and join the movement.

The role of women in early Christianity exemplifies the "elective affinity" principle in the development of a religious movement (Weber 1968, 488–90; Collins 1975, 244–46). In the international market economy of the Roman Empire, many women through their own commercial activities achieved lower-middle-class occupational status for the first time. Their rise in economic position generated a new consciousness of gender equality with men. Unlike Judaism or the mystery religions, early Christianity accepted women in full and equal membership. There was thus an affinity of interests between the Christian pastors and evangelists who were seeking converts for their ascetic spiritual movement and lower-middle-class women who sought an egalitarian religious home. The appeal of early Christianity to women and their participation was a major factor in its spread, and conversely, the position of women in the church contributed to their further economic and status gains in this period.[3]

Max Weber's "Protestant ethic" thesis is a notable example of the elective affinity approach in the sociology of religion. If one were enumerating the reasons that pastoral caregivers ought to be interested in sociology, one reason high on the list would certainly be that the subject of Weber's famous book, *The Protestant Ethic and the Spirit of Capitalism,* is pastoral care.

Seventeenth-century Reformed church pastors faced a difficult pastoral problem, Weber observed, when confronted by anxious parishioners. The source of the problem was Calvin's teaching about predestination. In his theology, Calvin emphasized the absolute sovereignty of God and concluded from this doctrine that human works have no power to affect the person's salvation. Calvin stressed that there is no discernible earthly sign differentiating the "elect" and the "damned." While Calvin had no question about his own soteriological status, his followers faced the awful dilemma of realizing the supreme importance of salvation while having no visible way of knowing their status. The Calvinist pastors, giving counsel to their troubled congregants, advised that while there was no unambiguous way to discern one's election, nevertheless certain signs were very suggestive of God's blessing: the absence of sin, a lifestyle of diligence, thrift, and self-denial, and worldly prosperity. Weber characterized this ethos as "worldly ascetism," a rational ethic of economic activity coupled with nonconsumption. This ethos, from an economic point of view, was the spirit of early capitalism, for it stressed saving, reinvestment of profit into the industry, and the rationalization of the whole economic process.

A modern application of the "elective affinity" concept has been suggested by sociologist of religion J. Alan Winter (1977, 43–78), who sees a similar "fit" between the ideology of modern corporation management and modern theology. The manager today working in a large organization coordinates many experts whose specific work he or she does not understand. Modern management thus stresses human interrelationships and building high motivation among teams of specialists. A principal virtue of good managers is humility, not taking personal credit for the group's accomplishments. An "elective affinity" exists between this ideology of management and process theology. Process theology stresses the idea of the interdependence of the individual and a loving God in the performance of a common task. Unlike the old Protestant ethic, which clearly subordinated the individual to God, process theology views God and the individual as equals, mutually dependent upon each other. God and individuals become coworkers with much the same relationship as managers and their work teams.

Progressive Secularization

The transformation of a religious community from the original charismatic movement to the later institutionalized establishment represents a process of secularization. Here we recall our earlier definition of secularization as a shrinkage in the role of religion in social life and in individual consciousness. The routinization of charisma and the process of elective affinity cause a reduction both in the tension between the religious community and the existing social order and in the conflict between the movement's theological vision and the society's dominant worldview. The radical otherworldliness of the early religion is delegitimized as "idealistic," "impractical," "impossible."

Sociologists of religion use the broad terms *sect* and *church* to refer to the less and more secularized types of religious communities (Johnson 1963). For the sect, there is significant tension between the religious organization and the larger society. For the church, this tension is minimal. Christianity first crossed this sect-church threshold in its transition under Constantine from persecuted religious movement to dominant religiocultural order.

Schism and Revival

It is significant that the secularization of religious communities results in internal conflict that causes the regeneration of sectarian movements. Not only do sects become churches but churches have an inherent tendency to spawn sects. Rodney Stark and William Bainbridge (1985, 1987) formulate an important theory of secularization, schism, and revival to address the dynamics of this reaction to secularization. Daniel Bell (1977) offers a parallel theory of resistance to secularization, a process he terms "resacralization."

Stark and Bainbridge ground their theory in a social psychological understanding of religion. These sociologists of religion assert that religion involves what they call *compensators*, that is, "beliefs that a reward will be obtained in the distant future or in some other context which cannot be immediately verified" (1985, 6). There are two types of compensators. *Specific compensators* are empirical in the sense that they can be verified within a certain period of time, as for example when parents tell their children that if they work hard, they will get good jobs and be successful. *General compensators* such as finding cosmic meaning or achieving eternal life are nonempirical (that is, beyond scientific proof) and thus involve beliefs about supernatural or transcendent reality. Secular or naturalistic "religions," because they lack the transcendent dimension, do not provide credible general compensators, thus making them less appealing than transcendent religions in the religious economy.

Stark and Bainbridge combine their conception of transcendent religion as a general compensator and Weber's idea of the routinization of charisma. Over time, religious sects lose their transcendental orientation as they become accommodated to the social environment. As we have seen, they become churches, adapted to the existing culture and its dominant values. This transformation causes the belief system of the now-secularized sect-become-church to lose its reward value as a general compensator. Conflict results between the members of the religious community most sensitive to the loss of transcendence and other members less sensitive to this loss. The dissatisfied members become part of a *schism* and pull out of the church, charging that the church has become "worldly" and that it has betrayed its transcendent raison d'être. These members form the nucleus of *revival*, which is the formation of a new sect-type religious organization that stresses the tension with the dominant social environment. But then, over time, this organization becomes secularized too, and the process repeats. Thus, in figure 5-1, the relationship of progressive secularization, schism, and revival is represented as cyclical.

In the religious economy, Stark and Bainbridge argue that secularization is and has always been a constant process, but that secularization is only one of three religious dynamics at work. Revival is the second, the reaction of persons *within* the progressively more secularized religious organizations whose need for transcendence is sacrificed and who split off to form new *sects*. *Innovation* is the third process, the reaction to the general secularized atmosphere of persons *outside* the specific religious organizations who form *cults* to establish the supernatural encounter. In our contemporary American religious context, Stark and Bainbridge understand the current conservative and fundamentalist movements in the established churches to exemplify the revival process, while the explosion of esoteric groups demonstrates the innovation process. Both processes, however, have their root in the same human need for credible general compensators. Stark and Bainbridge's theory is based on the same observation Berger makes that secularization does not represent a change in human consciousness but does represent the delegitimation of religious experience.

Understanding secularization as a pervasive dynamic of every religious organization over time helps us assess recent developments in the American religious scene since Dean Kelley published his widely read book, *Why Conservative Churches Are Growing* (1972). The rapid growth of some of those conservative churches, for example, the Assemblies of God, has slowed sharply. A recent study (Tinlin and Blumhofer 1991) shows the increased accommodation to the secular world and reduced fervor of this denomination's pentecostal churches. I encountered earlier evidence of this accommodation in the late 1970s when I visited a large and prosperous midwestern Assemblies church, where the senior pastor told the members of the city's ministerial association not to expect the old-fashioned charismatic vitality in its worship services.

An argument parallel to that of the sociologists of religion is made by several theologians surveying the present religious situation. Extremely forceful is Morton Kelsey, who develops a modern theology of Christian experience (1972) and has shown its implications for pastoral care (1982). Kelsey recounts the incidence of youth's involvement in occult and cult activity. Then he says, youth *of course* will be attracted to cults because the secularization of the churches and the dominance of rational materialism in established religious circles closes off their access to transcendental religion. Renewal of transcendent religious consciousness, what Stark and Bainbridge would call revival, is the only hope Kelsey feels we have to win back the younger generation to the churches.

The model of the dynamics of religious communities presented in this section reveals something of the complexity of alienating and de-alienating religion. The routinization of charisma and the process of progressive secularization, which reduce the tension between religion and world, represent the alienation process, while the original charismatic community and the processes of schism and revival show the possibility of de-alienation. This model, which joins classical and contemporary approaches to sociology of religion, provides an important theoretical basis for the effort of pastoral care to support the careseeker's quest of de-alienating religion. The practical application of this model to the pastoral care process occupies our attention in the last section of this chapter.

However, before we can attend successfully to the implications of the sociology of religion for understanding and aiding *careseekers*, we must look at its implications for bringing into focus the *caregivers*. The model of the dynamics of religious communities has much to say about the different ways pastoral care is conceived and carried out. Related to the sociology of the dynamics of religious communities that we have just reviewed is a corollary sociology of modern theology. Since pastoral care is a practical theological discipline, this latter thrust of the sociology of religion has high relevance. The inductive mode of pastoral care advocated in this book has its roots in this sociology of modern theological method.

Sociology of Modern Theological Method

Peter Berger, in his important book *The Heretical Imperative: Contemporary Possibilities of Religious Affirmation* (1979), identifies three broad types of theological response to the problem of religion in the modern society. Berger terms these modern "possibilities" of religious affirmation the "deductive," the "reductive," and the "inductive." These three methods of theological reflection are different solutions to the tension between the original religious hierophany, which as we said was the immediate experience of divine revelation, together with its formulation in holy scripture, on the one hand, and the modern worldview on the other hand. As a sociologist of religion, Berger finds these three responses in all religious faiths confronting modernism, although his major exposition relates to Protestant Christianity.

Figure 5-2 represents the historic relationship of these three modern theological options to the charismatic origins of the particular religious community.

Berger contrasts the three modern theological options with the dominant theological method in the premodern period, *orthodoxy*. He has medieval Catholicism and premodern Islam primarily in mind here. The premodern societies reflecting orthodoxy had religious stability based on the interlocking association of worldview and ethos, using Clifford Geertz's terms. Taken-for-granted external authority and the believer's internal certainty reinforced each other. Thus the five times daily calls to prayer from the Islamic minarets were answered in the devout Muslim's consciousness by a subjective antiphony, "Yes, it is so, and it can be no other."

The *modern situation* intervenes as a giant obstacle to the smooth flow of religious orthodoxy. The social psychology of modernity, such as Berger's "homeless mind," massively disrupts the subjective antiphony of orthodox believers. Urban life, pluralism of worldviews, the onslaught of Enlightenment and scientific thought, and the secularization of societies make impossible for most modern people the religious certainty of the premodern believer.

Berger's three modern theological options are responses to the disruption by the modern situation of religious consciousness. The *deductive* theological option "deduces" from the hierophanic religious vision as represented in the canonic writings the appropriate attitudes, behaviors, and organizational forms for modern believers. Examples of this method are such neo-orthodox and neo-traditional movements as Karl Barth's Protestantism and Islamic fundamentalism. The revelation of God is an objective "given." The only acceptable attitude to the revelation is obedience:

> The proper task of theological reflection is not to meet the arguments of unbelief or to produce arguments of its own on behalf of belief but to clarify the contents of the revelation that has already been given to faith. (Berger 1979, 75)

The neo-orthodox response denies the importance of the cognitive challenges from modern experience. Yet the inner antiphony of the premodern orthodox believers cannot be easily reproduced in the modern situation. The antiphony has been broken, and its contemporary equivalent can only be: "Yes, I have heard this before; but it *could* be other; is it really so?" Neo-orthodox religion, because it affirms the tradition *anew*, after a period when it was not affirmed, has a particular vehemence, necessary to drown out recollections of the interval of nonobservance.

In a critique of the neo-orthodox option, Berger observes that no person's process of religious commitment can be viewed only

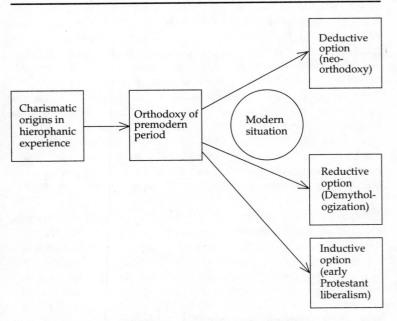

FIG. 5-2. Theological responses to the modern situation

from the standpoint of a religious vision's objective truth. Always there is a subjective process of decision involving influences and values that lead to a particular commitment. Berger notes the inconsistency in Barth's term "dialectical theology," for Barth steadfastly refused to look at the subjective aspects of his autobiography and reactions that led him to make the "leap of faith" in the direction of conservative Protestant Christianity.

The second theological response, the *reductive* option, "reduces" the original religious vision to the dimensions of the modern worldview. In contrast to the deductive response, which sees the historic revelation as the "given," the reductive option sees modern culture as given and as superior to archaic cultures. This is the point of view discussed earlier that takes for granted that modern consciousness represents a pinnacle from which all other epistemologies can be surveyed. A process of what Berger calls "cognitive bargaining" characterizes the reductive method, as when some Christians reject Jesus' miracle of feeding the five thousand as implausible but insist on keeping the bodily resurrection. Rudolf Bultmann's program of demythologization of the Christian gospel is Berger's prime example of the reductive possibility. All elements of the tradition that are deemed incompatible with the cognitive assumptions of modernity are abandoned. The reductive goal is to discover and communicate the central religious core stripped of what to the modern mind are its dubious historical trappings. As is well known, Bultmann claimed the basic Christian truth, its kerygma, was this: Human beings cannot free themselves of their own accord from the anguish of their condition and must rely on God's action to do so. The central casualty of the reductive method is the sense of divine transcendence.

Berger uses the sociology of knowledge to critique the reductive method. Its fallacy, Berger holds, is the assumption that modern consciousness represents a cognitive pinnacle. Each historical era has a distinctive mode of consciousness, and any change from one era to another involves cognitive gains and losses. The reductive method assumes that modern human beings are incapable of freely choosing their worldview. It mistakenly asserts that certain perspectives are cognitively impossible for modern people to employ (such as a mythological worldview). A truly adequate theological method, Berger asserts, respects the capability of mature modern people to construct a worldview that combines epistemological elements of different historic worldviews so as to overcome the cultural myopia so characteristic of modernity.

The *inductive* option, the third of Berger's types, "induces" from human experience and its religious intuitions the vital questions whose answers may be sought in the religious tradition of the hierophanic vision. Central to the inductive method is the recognition of the choice-making individual in modernity. As we noted earlier, in religion as in other spheres, modern people no longer experience a world where religious worldviews are determined by fate of birth into a particular community but rather an environment where choices are confronted on all sides. While the deductive method focuses totally on the "objective" revelation, the inductive method gives attention both to the subjective experience of the searcher and to the religious traditions.

Berger's primary exemplar of the inductive option is Friedrich Schleiermacher, the pioneer of modern Protestant liberalism. Others representing this method are Ernst Troeltsch, Rudolf Otto, and William James. Schleiermacher's bombshell book, *On Religion: Speeches to Its Cultured Despisers* (1968 [1799]), rejects dogmatics and ethics as the core of religion in favor of human beings' intuitive knowledge of their dependence on the Absolute. Religious intuition propels the search for an adequate religious belief-system. Because religious truth differs from scientific knowledge and ethical principles, nonmodern worldviews have equal potential validity in terms of religious adequacy. Schleiermacher was accused of turning theology into anthropology, the study of God into the study of human beings. Berger believes this is a mistaken understanding of Schleiermacher, who only *started* his theological reflection with experience. Schleiermacher engaged in a serious search of the different religious traditions, evaluating belief-systems for their adequacy as answers to deep human religious intuitions. As Berger and also Williams (1978) stress, Schleiermacher's theology is bipolar, working from both the pole of human experience and the pole of the Christ of biblical tradition. As Berger notes, from our present-day stance, we can justly say that Schleiermacher did not give fair treatment to certain non-Christian traditions, especially Judaism. However, for Berger's purposes (and ours), what is crucial is Schleiermacher's method of theological response to the challenge of modernism.

It is useful to compare the model of dynamics of religious communities represented in figure 5-1 and Berger's model of the sociology of theological options in figure 5-2. Orthodoxy in the latter model represents the premodern stage of secularization as depicted in figure 5-1 as the routinization of charisma and the phase of elective affinity. The modern *reductive* option corresponds to the progressive secularization phase of religious communities. This stance reduces the tension between theology and the modern world to a minimum. The modern *deductive* and *inductive* options both express the thrusts of modern religious communities toward schism and revival. Central for both is the reaffirmation of divine transcendence, an idea eclipsed in the dominant modernist worldview. The deductive method as seen in neo-orthodox theology accomplishes this reaffirmation by extremely focused attention on the charismatic origins of the religious movements and the extant descriptions of the initial hierophanic experience. The inductive method seeks to balance the subjective and objective sources of religious truth by correlating the experience of the modern believer and the traditions of religious revelation.

An Inductive Approach to Pastoral Care

The definition of pastoral care used in this book, as a dialogue exploring the possibility and implications of a religious definition of the careseeker's situation, has its main roots in the inductive approach to theological reflection outlined by Berger. Each of the three theological options—Berger's contemporary possibilities for religious affirmation—forms the basis for a mode of pastoral care. Few pastors or chaplains use one method exclusively, but each caregiver has a more or less predominant style. Here we look briefly at these different pastoral approaches and evaluate them from the viewpoint of the sociology of religion.

Pastors and others ministering out of the deductive or neo-orthodox perspective stress the word of God and scriptural Christian responses. Subjective reactions are subordinated to faithful observance, as when persons grieving a loss through death are enjoined to feel joy about the loved one's new life in heaven. In the neo-orthodox mode, the Christian caregiver has the duty of clearly articulating the gospel as it applies to the careseeker's situation but is not responsible for the careseeker's response. Jesus' injunction to the disciples to shake off the dust of the villages where their message was unwelcome is consistent with the neo-orthodox style of pastoral care.

There are strengths and weaknesses of the neo-orthodox style of pastoral care. Because it emphasizes the objective level and denies what is going on at the subjective level, the neo-orthodox style is welcomed by some persons who are "hopelessly torn up inside" by conflicting emotions. To careseekers overcome by our age of subjectivity, the neo-orthodox approach comes as a breath of fresh air—"Finally someone will tell me what to believe." But submission to a powerful and confident voice, whether of the pastor or of the tradition, requires the continuous exertion of will to keep the contrary inner voices repressed. After the crisis period passes, careseekers often resent their "escape from freedom" through submission to authority.

Strong institutional pressures limit the amount of pastoral care conducted from the deductive viewpoint in hospitals and other care centers. Violating the canons of tolerance for different religious viewpoints, of personal privacy, and of attention to feelings and subjective states, caregivers who operate from this perspective are screened out of chaplaincy staffs and, as pastors visiting hospital patients, they are restricted by nursing and pastoral care personnel from involvement with any patients not directly affiliated with their congregations.

The reductive option is represented in much contemporary pastoral care. Caregivers operating from this viewpoint accept the pluralism and secularization of modern consciousness as a given. Religion is understood in functional terms as an aid that some people employ to cope with life and crisis. Here the adage, "Different strokes for different folks," represents an orienting theme. The approach is pragmatic in the sense that whatever belief-system gets people from day to day (without significantly harming others) is deemed to have validity. Certain emphases characterize this style of pastoral care including caregivers being agenda-free, supporting people along the path *they* have chosen, and being nonjudgmental. The individualistic ethos of modern society influences the reductive style of pastoral care. This ethos encourages the ideas that people have a right to their own beliefs, religion is not for everybody, and anyway, the historical religious traditions carry a lot of problematic baggage. Pastoral caregivers who manifest a strong reductive tendency often take a "clinical" or scientific stance toward a careseeker's religious ideation, a watchful attitude of "Let's see how much good religion does for this person."

The inductive approach in pastoral care gives primary emphasis to the choices facing careseekers regarding adequate worldviews. Its starting point is the experience, often a crisis, of the congregant, patient, or counselee. Pastoral conversation from this perspective begins with the careseeker's definition of the situation. The full subjectivity of the person's crisis is elicited and enlarged. From the outset, however, the inductive pastor recognizes the individual's interpretation of his or her situation as involving critical choices, generally unconscious, among alternative definitions of the situation. Careseekers, unaware that their perceptions of the crisis or problem are social constructions of reality, choices based on complex influences, often experience a depressive feeling of fixity, "stuckness," and "No Exit." The inductive pastoral approach heightens the careseeker's sense of freedom about definitions of the situation. Its hallmark is the dethronement of modern Western enlightenment thought from its vaunted position of cognitive supremacy. To use an overworked current phrase, inductive pastoral care creates a level playing field for the competition of different modes of consciousness. Religious consciousness assumes a viability in inductive pastoral care that is lacking when considered only in terms of the modernist mentality of rational materialism.

The inductive approach, in short, assigns major importance to the modern social context of pastoral care. To use Berger's phrase, that context creates the "heretical imperative" for the careseeker. The context impels choice-making among alternative worldviews where orthodoxies no longer are determinative. Compared to a deductive style, the inductive approach to pastoral care stresses the dialogical character of pastoral interaction and does not suppress full realization of modernism's challenge to religious viewpoints. Compared to a reductive style, the inductive approach grants legitimacy to different modes of consciousness and encourages careseekers to live in different cognitive worlds. Its goal is constructing from the several available worldviews the one most adequate for understanding the careseeker's situation.

Alienating Religion and Breadth
of Perspective: A Key to De-alienation

One further concept from the sociology of religion, *a person's breadth of perspective*, must be considered before we can move to this chapter's final section, the applications of this viewpoint to work with careseekers.

We have indicated in this chapter that pastoral caregivers are generally interested in encouraging de-alienating religion in careseekers, religion that does not legitimate racist, classist, authoritarian, and patriarchal social structures. Sociological research, it was noted earlier, consistently finds a correlation between religious orthodoxy and support for conservative political ideologies. Orthodoxy in these surveys means agreement with traditional beliefs about God, Christ, and transcendence. This association of orthodoxy and prejudice is frequently observed by hospital chaplains, for they have pastoral conversations with a very large number of people who—because the chaplain is a stranger and not in the same authority relationship to them as their pastor—present "unscreened" viewpoints. Commonly, patients tell the chaplain about their strong Christian religious beliefs but a few minutes later in the conversation, they are talking in extremely prejudicial terms about gender and ethnic groups and about the breakdown of society because of affirmative action, the criminal element, welfare chiseling, and working mothers.

The sociology of religion sheds significant light on this correlation between religious orthodoxy and political authoritarianism. At first, this correlation was thought to indicate a *causal* relationship between orthodoxy and authoritarianism, the former causing the latter. Later, however, more sophisticated techniques of factor analysis revealed that the relationship between orthodoxy and authoritarianism was *spurious* (Roof 1978, 170–78). In other words, the apparent relationship between these two variables—religious orthodoxy and political conservatism—is caused by the impact of another variable.

An example of a spurious relationship that I like to use with sociology students is the correlation between the number of fire trucks that go to a fire and the amount of damage caused by the fire. The more fire trucks that go to the fire, the greater the damage. The erroneous conclusion one could draw is that the fire trucks *cause* the damage. The correlation between number of fire trucks and damage is a spurious relationship, for there is, of course, no causal relationship. Both the number of fire trucks and the amount of damage are the effects of the true cause, the size of the fire.

The causal factor that explains the apparent but spurious relationship between religious orthodoxy and alienating religion is the person's *breadth of perspective*, as it is termed by sociologist W. Clark Roof (Roof 1978, 181–200; Carroll, Dudley, McKinney 1986, 54). In chapter 3 this factor was implicit in the discussion of a person's reference group orientation, localism or cosmopolitanism. On the attitudinal continuum of breadth of perspective, locals are low and cosmopolitans are high. The locals, persons with narrow or low breadth of perspective, tend to conceive of social reality in fixed, absolute terms. The cosmopolitans, those having wider or high breadth of perspective, see the social order as a human construction open to change. Some association exists between higher educational level and wider breadth of perspective. Persons rated higher in localism (narrow breadth of perspective) tend to have religious beliefs that include many extrinsic factors, that is, cultural trappings not integrally related to basic theology. The religious beliefs of cosmopolitans, on the other hand, are more intrinsic, oriented to the theological core issues.

> The more limited the social perspective, the less church members are constrained to develop integrated, theologically based belief systems. Considering the crucial part that a person's breadth of perspective plays, a fundamental observation about belief systems should be noted: historic theological doctrines are always filtered through the believer's cultural experience. (Roof 1978, 175)

Thus, de-alienating religion (less supportive of a conservative social order of hierarchy, patriarchy, and authoritarianism) rests on the foundation of a wider breadth of perspective characteristic of the more cosmopolitan person.

Breadth of perspective is a basic personality characteristic, not a trait that a person easily changes. If pastoral caregivers want to encourage de-alienating religion in careseekers, they must realize that alienating religion is an expression of this basic personality characteristic. Therefore, change toward de-alienating religion depends upon the person gradually experiencing a change of consciousness in the direction of wider breadth of perspective. How might pastoral caregivers encourage this latter transformation? It is helpful here to remember a central sociological axiom: *new actions precede new attitudes*. If we cause people to behave in new ways, their new actions create cognitive dissonance that puts strain on their old attitudes, and their attitudes change toward consistency with their new behaviors. For instance, we can require persons in interracial situations to behave in nondiscriminatory ways through the use of strong social sanctions (that is, good enforcement). Research finds that when this happens, individuals' new nondiscriminatory behavior creates mental tension with their prejudiced racial attitudes. The result is accommodation of the attitudes to correspond with the new behaviors, prejudiced attitudes changing to greater acceptance.

We will look at the implications of breadth of perspective for pastoral care when we turn to the applications of the sociology of religion. What is important about this theoretical and technical discussion is that factor analysis of data on alienating religion provides evidence that it is *not* caused by religious orthodoxy. Orthodox people—those who believe in transcendent Christianity—who have wide breadth of perspective are likely to manifest dealienating religious views, opposing racism, sexism, and a hierarchical economic and social order.

Applying the Sociology of Religion to the Care Process

In a previous section, we examined how the sociology of religion sheds light on the different approaches of pastoral caregivers. Now in this final section, we must look at how the sociology of religion illuminates the careseeker's situation and the interaction between caregiver and careseeker. This sociological perspective helps the work of pastoral caregivers in four main ways.

First, the sociology of religion helps us do pastoral assessment. This is the initial pastoral diagnosis of the careseeker's problem. Pastoral assessment asks what is the careseeker's definition of the situation. This definition is an expression of the careseeker's larger worldview. Pastoral assessment involves a characterization of that worldview in terms of its religious dimensions and assumptions. This worldview is not a static phenomenon, of course, but is dynamic in the sense of incorporating the modern cognitive tensions we have reviewed.

The sociological dynamics of religious communities in the modern situation mirror the psychological dynamics of careseekers. In other words, the model of dynamics of religious communities represented in figure 5-1 is the externalization in people's behavior of their internal psychic struggle. The cycle of progressive secularization, schism, and revival in religious communities has its psychological counterpart in the careseeker's mental cycle of progressive absorption in modern consciousness, restlessness over that mentality's delegitimation of religious experience, and achievement of a sense of transcendence. But that achievement is constantly challenged by the everpresent assault of modern consciousness. Similarly, the careseeker's inner dynamics reflect Berger's sociological model of modern theology in figure 5-2. The careseeker's soul encompasses the debate over the orthodox, deductive, reductive, and inductive options for religion.

Let us observe how this viewpoint changes the way a hypothetical caregiver, Pastor Bob, understands the members of his congregation. Pastor Bob's present image of his parishioners is static. He has developed a little typology to categorize them. There are three groups, he says, in this largely white middle-class Protestant congregation in a racially integrated urban area of a midwestern city: the Spirituals, the Seculars, and the Traditionals. The Spirituals want strongly transcendent religion, focusing on prayer, Bible study, and the gifts of the Spirit. Traditional Protestant worship is too staid and emotionally subdued for these members. Some of the Spirituals feel a kinship with African-American religion and desire greater racial integration of the church. The Seculars are men and women, often working in management positions, whose goal is the "well-run" church. Their primary objectives are good administration and good fellowship. This group has hard workers who focus on such "here and now" projects as church building programs and social affairs. The Seculars express class attitudes toward the neighborhood when they welcome middle-class African Americans who "appreciate our style of church." The Traditionals are mostly older people who remember the church as a community center. Their religious attitude is somewhere between the Spirituals and the Seculars, a mixture of transcendence and culture. They appreciate the old-time church hymns, choir anthems, and prayers. Among this group, pastors are put on a pedestal. Social change is disconcerting to the Traditionals, especially the prospect of changes in the church to be inclusive of the African-American neighborhood population and to support the leadership of women.

Pastor Bob's understanding of his congregation changes from a static to a dynamic picture when informed by the sociology of religion. The forces of secularization, schism, and revival are constantly at work in a congregation. Also, and here is where the congregation's sociological dynamics mirror the member's psychological dynamics, these forces are constantly in tension within the parishioner's soul. Thus, the Seculars have modern consciousness as a dominant attitudinal motif but also encompass the viewpoint of the Spirituals and the Traditionals as "minority" voices. Evidence for this is the intensity of church conflicts, which demonstrate strong defense mechanisms of reaction formation and projection of the unassimilated voices. The Spirituals, unable to accept their own Seculars, reveal strong anger against their Secular fellow parishioners. The intensity of the Seculars' anger toward the Spirituals may be stronger still, for their own internal Spiritual receives little cultural affirmation. Traditionals are torn in both directions, toward more religion and toward less, hence their feeling of resistance to change.

Thus, as the first contribution of the sociology of religion to pastoral care, we see how the caregiver's pastoral assessment of the "living human document" sitting adjacent in the pastor's office is informed by the sociology of religion's dynamic view of religious communities and their underlying psychological tensions. The careseeker may sound "secular" but that often masks the delegitimation of religious experience. Conversely, the highly "spiritual" careseeker is in tension with strong secularizing forces from without and within.

Second, the sociology of religion helps us understand the "fit" between the worldviews of caregivers and careseekers. The dynamic understanding of religion as a resultant of conflicting forces helps explain the rapport that caregivers feel with certain careseekers and the tension they experience with others. Parishioners, hospital patients, and counselees are suspicious of caregivers who are not members of their "group." Conversely, each pastor, chaplain, or counselor identifies more strongly with one group than another. A pastor's counseling will tend to be focused within his or her accustomed group, because of the good "vibes" exchanged. In hospital ministry, this selective process begins in the "getting acquainted" phase when caregiver and careseeker meet for the first time and engage in mutual exploration of general attitudes toward religion. Patients scrutinize chaplains for cues about how "religious" they are. The "Spirituals" want high religiosity, the "Seculars" want low. At the same time, chaplains are happy to find signs of religious compatibility in patients. For example, one caregiver, very oriented to process theology, leans toward a theology of immanence rather than transcendence. He finds that he cannot minister effectively to some patients because of their more conservative orientation.

The case of Harold illustrates the selective process that brings together like-minded caregivers and careseekers. It also shows how careseekers endeavor to structure their world in order to protect their worldview. Harold, a married high school teacher in his early forties, with four children, is a nonsmoker hospitalized for lung cancer with metastasis to the spine. He is receiving both radiation and chemotherapy treatments. Harold and his family attend a conservative nondenominational Protestant church. Harold is concerned about the attitude of hospital staff members toward his prospects for recovery. The chaplain assigned to the hospital unit, who is a strong believer in spiritual healing, is welcomed by Harold as a caregiver. Several nurses who share a positive attitude about Harold's chances for survival become his favorite nursing personnel. They are regularly assigned to care for him. The hospital unit's psychological counselor, popular with many of the patients, is politely but firmly rejected by Harold because of his "negative" attitude. Harold eventually dies. When near death, he expresses his belief that he survived as long as he did—beyond the oncologists' expectations—because of the prayer, spiritual support, and positive atmosphere maintained both at home and in the hospital.

This case illustrates how persons may very self-consciously build plausibility structures that help them sustain religious definitions of the situation, definitions not supported by the dominant culture. Understood in the context of the dynamics of religious communities, Harold's behavior toward the hospital staff exemplifies the schism and revival phases of the religious dynamics model. Harold rejects secularized attitudes and separates himself from the people who do not share his transcendent perspective. The chaplain reinforces his religious definition of the situation. Harold's behavior in the pastoral care setting is sectarian, against conformity with the dominant medical social environment. The case of Harold thus illustrates this second contribution of the sociology of religion perspective to pastoral care: its illumination of the religious dynamics of the interaction between the caregiver and the careseeker.

Third, the sociology of religion helps us encourage de-alienating religion in careseekers, religion that does not legitimate racist, authoritarian, or patriarchal social structures. The key determinant of de-alienating religion is wide breadth of perspective. What is the implication of the central role of breadth of perspective for pastoral care? How might pastoral caregivers support careseekers' growth toward greater breadth of perspective, which in turn would cause them to be more responsive to alternative religious definitions less culturally captive and more theologically informed?

Developing strategies to widen careseekers' breadth of perspective requires the caregiver to give serious consideration to the way new actions precede new attitudes. Broader social experience is the pathway to wider breadth of perspective. Submersion in new cultural milieus causes cognitive dissonance between the new observations and the old mentality, and resolution of the tension is achieved through attitudinal change.

Pastoral caregivers need to use imagination in structuring learning contexts for adults similar to those used by Christian educators working with children and youth. The latter make consistent application of the principle of contextual learning. They recognize that a work camp experience in a third-world country has a powerful effect in widening the breadth of perspective of a church's youth group. A junior year abroad (preferably high school but also college) has a still greater impact. In the pastoral care of adults, the theme of one contextual approach is "social action as pastoral care." Careseekers who are recruited to serve breakfast to homeless people in an inner-city outreach program experience the double benefit of doing something socially useful and widening their breadth of perspective. "Bible study as pastoral care" is another such theme, the Old Testament and New Testament texts being seriously investigated in small groups for their message to the original hearers. This process achieves not only religious learning but also stretches the participants' minds to deal with alternative modes of consciousness, thus widening breadth of perspective.

Thus, the sociology of religion perspective makes this third contribution to pastoral care of providing a general orientation for addressing the problem of alienating religion. By seeing such religion as an outgrowth of narrow breadth of perspective and by considering how basic attitudinal change depends upon new behaviors, caregivers realize the importance of experimenting with unusual care modalities.

Fourth, the sociology of religion causes pastoral care to recognize the social matrix that shapes the careseeker's religious worldview. Persons' positions in the social structure constitute this matrix within which their understanding of God originates. This is Weber's idea of the "elective affinity" between social roles and theological viewpoints.

Being theologically trained, pastoral caregivers assume that the careseeker's social relations ought to reflect his or her theology. The sociology of religion demonstrates that the reverse process is at work, people's theology being shaped by their social relations. The sociological perspective is especially useful in understanding what is often called "popular religion." The religion of the poor and disenfranchised often posits the existence of many spiritual intermediaries between the individual and God. In Catholic popular religion, these intermediaries include the saints, the baby Jesus, and Mary. Pastoral caregivers working with careseekers whose religion stresses the mediating role of these spiritual beings frequently wonder why such persons in their prayers and devotions find it difficult to visualize direct encounters with God. The key to understanding lies in the social experience of the poor. In his book informed by the sociology of religion, *Constructing Local Theologies*, Robert Schreiter writes:

> Images of God, of Christ, of Mary reflect other social relationships in a person's life. The image of Christ as brother may work in a middle-class setting where one is in a position to initiate all kinds of voluntary associations, but not in class situations where the powerful are feared and distrusted. (1985, 140)

People's understanding of the divine-human encounter mirrors their experience of the economic class structure.

Grasping this "elective affinity" between social viewpoint and theological viewpoint reorients pastoral care. Changes in persons' social relationships yield transformation in their theology rather than vice versa. Schreiter puts it this way:

> The Marxist analysts are probably right when they say that the world-view and patterns of popular religion cannot be changed without a concomitant change in the economic relations. Religious symbols will continue to mirror, however obliquely, other relationships within the lives of people. (1985, 140)

Realizing the importance of power relationships as a matrix for the shaping of theology creates a further impetus for caregivers to work for careseekers' empowerment in the social system.

A pastoral encounter in the hospital illustrating how the social situation shapes theology remains strongly etched in my memory. A girl in her late teens had suffered a broken neck in an automobile accident. She faced the prospect of being a quadriplegic. Speaking to her several days after the accident, I realized she firmly believed the accident and whatever disability she faced were the will of God. This theology was abhorrent to me, and I contested her view of God and its implications, suggesting this theology made God into a cruel tyrant. My reaction was disturbing to her, and she let it be known that she did not want any further visits from me. Thinking about this afterward, I realized I had not taken her social situation into account. This teenage girl lived in a small town where social relationships in families, churches, and the community were highly structured. In recent years this town had been caught up in a maelstrom of economic and social change. Residents had the sense of their lives being changed by distant powers they did not understand. Realizing this was the social environment the young woman had experienced, I understood better how she could perceive God as being completely in control (her experience of fixity of social relationships) and yet be unfathomable (her experience of distant forces creating upsetting changes).

This example illustrates how the social situation is a matrix for the careseeker's religious worldview. Contrary to our usual assumption, we realize that transformations in people's religious worldviews often depend upon changes in their social situation. Empowerment in the socioeconomic world affects the theology of the empowered.

Conclusion

Our attention in this chapter has been focused on two central concepts in the sociology of religion, secularization and alienation. Rather than being a force marching inexorably onward, secularization is part of a dynamic of religious communities that also includes religious revival and innovation. The delegitimation of religious experience and the loss of transcendence create psychological stress for persons who cannot achieve cognitive integration, and this tension motivates the careseeker's quest for adequate worldviews. Alienating religion, which mystifies the social order and veils its human construction, was viewed in this chapter as a consequence of persons' breadth of perspective and thus likely to be changed by wider social experience. Secularization and alienation continue to occupy our attention in the next chapter, which focuses on the dilemmas of pastoral caregivers working in secular institutional contexts and their resolution.

6. The Institutional Context of Pastoral Care

The institutional contexts of modern pastoral care are highly diverse: congregations, pastoral counseling centers, general hospitals, long-term care facilities, mental hospitals, penitentiaries, schools and colleges, business and industry, military installations, even shopping malls. The diversity of settings has made it difficult for pastoral care to maintain a central focus when the situations of caregivers vary so greatly.

This chapter examines how the institutional context of pastoral care affects pastoral identity and its differentiation. If, as this book argues, the uniqueness of pastoral care compared with other therapeutic modalities is its exploration with careseekers of religious definitions of their situation, then we must inquire how that identity is affected by the organizational dynamics of the caregiver's institutional setting. Sociological perspectives from earlier chapters—modes of consciousness, reference groups, power structure, secularization—are marshalled here to shed light on the difficulties of pastoral existence in often alien territory.

The central concept employed in this chapter to analyze the caregiver's institutional stresses is *role conflict*. This sociological term refers to the situation whereby persons confront lack of consensus among their associates about their proper role. The sociological literature contains analyses of a number of occupations exposed to unusual degrees of role conflict: industrial foremen, waitresses, police officers, and the President of the United States (Palmer 1981). Employing this concept sheds significant light on a central dilemma of pastoral caregivers.

The chapter opens with a description of the broad institutional contexts of pastoral care in terms of dominant organizational cultures. This discussion sets the stage for the section on role conflict, where we analyze the tension between the expectations for pastoral care growing out of an organizational culture and the religious imperatives of pastoral care. This analysis of role conflict then leads into a section on the professionalization of pastoral care. At its heart, the professionalization controversy represents a role conflict struggle over the differentiation of pastoral identity. This struggle is examined in comparative perspective through a brief contrast of the pastoral care movements in the United States and Britain. Finally, we look at the implications of the role conflict perspective for achieving more highly differentiated pastoral care.

Although brief attention is given in this chapter to pastoral care in such other contexts as the military, the primary focus for this study of role conflict is the hospital situation and the way this institutional context impacts hospital chaplains. Highlighting the hospital environment serves two purposes. One is practical. From fourteen years of working in hospital settings, I am most familiar with the tensions in this institutional context. In fact, analyzing the role conflicts that my colleagues and I have faced in hospitals was a key impetus for writing this book. But the hospital case serves a theoretical purpose as well. The organizational culture of modern American hospitals, expressing what we will call the medical worldview, is a prime example of the dominant secular culture pervading the larger society. Hospitals are thus strategic research sites for studying the conflict of secular institutional expectations and the religious perspective of pastoral caregivers. Readers working in congregational and other institutional settings will recognize stresses similar to those of hospital chaplains in those other contexts.

Organizational Cultures

Organizational theory underwent a transformation in the 1970s, shifting from its preoccupation with the formal structure of business firms, governmental agencies, labor organizations, and voluntary associations (such as churches) to attention to their informal structure. The former concern with formal structure emphasized size, centralization, chain of command, and degree of bureaucratization. The newer interest in informal structure deals with less easily quantifiable factors: not the ideal world of organizational charts—how things are supposed to work—but the actual world of employee morale, interaction, and leadership. Studies done by such sociologists as Peter Blau (1963) had much earlier identified how informal structures often subverted the formal structures, but the import of these studies was not fully realized by the organizational theorists with economics and management backgrounds.

The "discovery" of organizations' informal structure in the seventies catapulted the perspective of organizational culture or "corporate culture" to the forefront of attention. After an incubation period in the academic literature, this perspective hit the popular media in the best-selling book, *In Search of Excellence: Lessons from America's Best-Run Companies*, by Tom Peters and Robert Waterman (1982). The authors advanced the thesis that the best corporations have "strong" cultures: common values shared by employees at all levels of the organization. The organizational culture point of view assumed prominence in the theological world in the new field of congregational studies, especially in James Hopewell's pathbreaking book, *Congregation* (1987), and its attention to congregational identity.

Organizational cultures exert influence upon the departments of the organization, conforming these units to its fundamental values, dynamics, and ethos. Of course, the organizational culture is not some impersonal force but is a definition of the situation carried in the heads of corporate officers, a standpoint enforced throughout the organization by means of policy and procedure manuals, department goals and objectives, and the reward structure for employee performance. These pressures toward standardization and conformity are all part of a larger trend of rationalization, a dominant characteristic of modern societies discerned by Weber.

Now we come to the central implication of organizational cultures for pastoral care. Because organizations operate for long-term survival in the secular world, their operational cultures are markedly secular in character, regardless of how lofty and spiritual their mission statements. Secularity here means this-worldly, culture-conforming, and oriented to the "bottom line." The cost-benefit calculus exerts a dominant influence over organizational life. This influence is the focus of *The Good Society* (1991) in which Robert N. Bellah and his colleagues trace how the cost-benefit mentality so pervades modern institutions as to eclipse other "lifeworld" values.

Organizational cultures, because of their secular and empirical character, stand in inevitable conflict with the religious perspective of pastoral care. The particular nature of the conflict varies depending on the particular institutional context of the caregiver. For example, local congregations operate in the organizational culture of a religious denomination with its traditional identity, its organizational structure, and the imperatives of institutional survival. The local church itself has an organizational culture that defines its particular identity and its operational goals. In the congregational context, pastoral caregivers may be under pressure to conform the care process to such institutional goals as membership growth or strategic targeting of particular groups.

Pastoral counseling centers have organizational cultures related to their special position in the mental health establishment of cities. This culture is shaped by relationships to the psychiatric community, area psychologists, community mental health centers, as well as local congregations. Institutional survival depends on cultivation of a network of referral agents. These agents comprise the reference group for pastoral counselors, and the agents' values—often secular in nature—represent pressures to give a particular "psychiatric" shape to pastoral counseling. In addition, maintaining the financial stability of pastoral counseling centers (a central organizational imperative) often conflicts with pastoral counselors' sense of the requirements of good client care.

The organizational cultures of governmental agencies often stand in dramatic tension with the perspective of pastoral care. Jails, penitentiaries, and other penal institutions are structured around philosophies of incarceration. Prison chaplains then find themselves at significant odds with this culture, when coercive control of inmates takes precedence over rehabilitation. Perhaps the classic case of potential institutional conflict for pastoral caregivers is that of the military chaplain, whose role conflict is discussed later in this chapter.

This cursory survey of different pastoral settings reveals the widespread possibility of tension generated by organizational cultures for pastoral caregivers. But what are the specific dynamics of conflict and how is the conflict resolved? To answer these questions, we will look again at the hospital as an institutional context for pastoral care. First, we need to contrast the organizational culture of hospitals with the perspective of pastoral care. Then we turn to the way caregivers resolve the resulting role conflict.

Lawrence Holst (1985) aptly describes the hospital chaplain as living "between worlds." Two cultures collide, and the pastoral caregiver stands in the middle. We will look primarily at three areas of conflict between the hospital's world and the pastoral world: relationships, suffering, and healing.

The organizational culture of large hospitals defines *relationships* in terms of hierarchical authority and formal rules. In contrast with other types of organizations, hospitals are highly bureacratic (Fox 1989). Unlike government bureaucracies, however, hospitals' authority structure and system of formal rules are subtle, for they project a community image of humanitarian personalism. While working as a hospital chaplain, I realized that a hospital had a different organizational culture in regard to staff relationships than the universities and local congregations where I had previously worked. Academic institutions, even the largest of them, are relatively open systems for faculty influence. "Chain of command" is not a firmly entrenched idea, and faculty and administrators talk freely without major preoccupation with anyone's rank. "Brought up," so to speak, in more democratic organizations of this type, I proceeded to act in much the same way as a new hospital chaplain in a large regional hospital. The administrator of the hospital was an accessible person, and I wrote her letters on several occasions identifying problems and recommending solutions. The administrator or the associate administrator wrote back thanking me and saying my letters had been passed on to the appropriate assistant administrators who handled the respective task areas. My letter about the visitor problem in the intensive care unit did not seem particularly different from the earlier ones, but this time, persons in the organizational chain of command informed me, quietly but strongly, that I had no business going directly to the top. The director of pastoral care is to be informed, who then discusses the issue with his or her assistant administrator, who then contacts the responsible assistant administrator, who sets up a fact-finding process, and if a problem is identified, an ad hoc committee is formed to propose a solution.

Hospitals' emphasis on hierarchy and formal rules conflicts with pastoral care's religious understanding of relationships. Caregivers oppose the impersonalism of systems in favor of personal concern for those abandoned or hurt. An egalitarianism pervades much pastoral theology in contrast with strongly hierarchical understandings of authority. Later in this chapter we will look closely at a controversy involving hospital rules.

Another important area of tension between the medical worldview dominating hospitals' organizational culture and the pastoral worldview concerns the issue of *suffering*. The medical "mission" is to vanquish suffering. The focus of the healing arts becomes the disease, not the person. Religion locates suffering in a larger context where its diminution, while important, is not the critical issue.

> The chaplain's theological perspective breeds cynicism about any medical efforts to banish suffering. Indeed, the chaplain has a prophetic word of caution to the medical community, namely, *that we not give suffering more than its due.* That caution would seek to remind that community that suffering is not infinite. Like us, like death, like angels and principalities, it is a creature. Like all creatures, it is subservient to the Creator. (Holst 1985, 25)

The complex issues of prolongation of life through advanced technology need not be discussed here. We need only note that medical personnel and pastoral caregivers often have markedly different understandings of suffering.

Another area of disagreement is attitudes toward *healing*. Although there has been significant change in the medical worldview concerning this issue, the dominant understanding continues to focus narrowly on persons' physical condition and neglect the emotional and spiritual dimensions. Pastoral care espouses an alternative holistic view of healing. This latter view encompasses a range of positions from support for adjunctive therapies developed by physicians and psychologists—Carl and Stephanie Matthews Simonton (1978) are good examples—to advocacy of divine healing centered on sacramental ministry linked to medical care (Payne 1989). The pioneers of modern healing ministry in the mainline churches, Agnes Sanford (1947, 1972) for example, encountered strong opposition from the medical establishment, and although diminished, the tension between the religious worldview and medical worldview continues.[1]

Alternative definitions of the situation, the organizational culture of hospitals on the one hand and the theological perspective of the chaplains on the other, could conceivably coexist on a basis of equality. Rarely is that the case. The power position of the spokespersons determines the hegemony of one perspective. In hospitals, the medical perspective has the dominant position, both because of the cultural ascendancy of the medical profession and because pastoral care departments do not contribute revenue, at least in a direct way, to the hospital's cost-benefit equation.

Living "between worlds" translates into a dilemma of organizational identity for hospital departments of pastoral care. Two broad strategies compete in chaplains' struggle to resolve the tension. On the one hand, the staff of a hospital's department of pastoral care seek a distinctive niche for their service in the competitive marketplace, where many "helping professionals" (social workers, psychologists, staff from psychiatry, and therapists of many varieties) all provide emotional and quasi-spiritual support for patients and their families. This "interest" pushes chaplains toward "product differentiation," toward advertising pastoral care as being markedly different from these other psychosocial services. On the other hand, in a day of radical cost-cutting by hospitals, when nonrevenue producing departments like pastoral care are being reduced if not eliminated, the job security interests of chaplains pushes them toward very safe and noncontroversial profiles in the hospital systems. Their survival instinct tells them to look very "straight" in terms of the dominant medical cognitive world. These two interests—product differentiation and noncontroversy—conflict, creating the chaplains' dilemma. The natural route of product differentiation for pastoral care is to stress the religious dimension of its "therapy," but it is just this dimension that puts pastoral care in conflict with the conventional scientific medical model of health care. That hospital pastoral care often seems to waver and vacillate in its style is due to an important degree to the tension between these competing strategies.

This discussion of organizational culture, the conflict between worldviews, and the strategic dilemma of pastoral care's identity in the organizational system sets the stage for an exploration in the next section of the dimensions and resolution of pastoral caregivers' role conflict.

Role Conflict

The concept of role is the central structural concept in all sociology. A role is the set of expectations that others have for the occupant of a social position. The role is a definition of the situation, the norms in people's heads about how clergypersons, physicians, mothers and fathers, astronauts, circus clowns, TV news anchorpersons, and Nobel Prize-winning scientists *ought* to act. Thus, the role as a set of norms differs from the actual behaviors of people, which obviously may deviate markedly from the expectations. To speak of social structure is to envision a society as a huge network of interlocking roles that give stability to the interactions of the society's members.

The concept of role has its origins in the theater, and the dramaturgical situation illustrates an important problem about roles. There may be a lack of consensus among the theater personnel about an actor's or actress's role. Should Willy Loman in *Death of a Salesman* be a tragic figure, a comic figure, or a pathetic figure? Different characterizations are possible and directors will differ in their expectations of the performer, depending upon their definition of the situation. This lack of consensus becomes even more pronounced in real-life social situations.

Role conflict occurs when there is lack of consensus among significant others regarding the expectations for an individual's proper role. Such disagreement represents a central source of confused identity for occupants of particular positions. Pastoral caregivers encounter significant role conflict growing out of differing expectations about their proper role. This is especially true in institutional settings where chaplains and other pastoral caregivers live between worlds.

Continuing the focus on hospital chaplains, we see in Raymond G. Carey's review (1985) of the results of surveys done at Lutheran General Hospital, Park Ridge, Illinois, the form role conflict assumes between the value-priorities of hospital chaplains and their constituencies: physicians, nurses, and patients. Factor analysis of the surveys delineates five major roles chaplains play: comforter, liturgist, witness, resource person, and counselor. The comforter role won highest regard from all groups, the chaplains and their role partners. There was agreement about the counselor role that was assigned lowest priority by all groups. However, there was marked difference of opinion regarding the other three roles. Chaplains saw their "witness" role as much more important than did the physicians, nurses, and patients; a greater proportion of chaplains responded positively to survey statements of role activity such as this: "To be present with patients and/or family in time of crisis as a *witness* of God's love and concern." The role partner groups assigned higher priority to the liturgist role than did the chaplains. A majority of physicians asked chaplains to confront the hospital administration on the ethical front regarding hospital policies or practices, while the chaplains assigned lower priority to this activity. Patients assigned low priority to chaplains' work of counsel or ethical guidance with hospital staff members.

Role conflict was defined above as lack of consensus about the individual's role among the person's significant others, those people who regularly interact with the position-occupant. The exact nature of the focal person's role conflict depends upon the values held by those role partners, and these values relate to the social positions the role partners occupy. Thus we can analyze role conflict by looking at the set of position-occupants who typically influence the occupant of the focal position. This is called the *role-set* (Merton 1957, 368–84). Figure 6-1 shows the role-set of a hospital chaplain. Of course, not all social workers, for example, have the same expectations of hospital chaplains, but their training and occupational culture give them a more or less common outlook. There is more consensus among a group of position-occupant partners than between that group and other groups. Thus, the role-set structures the role conflict of the hospital chaplain, with, for example, physicians sharing somewhat in common one set of expectations for the chaplains and social workers holding a different common set of expectations. Knowing the position of the person with whom she or he is interacting, the hospital chaplain develops an idea of what expectations that person will hold.

The findings of a definitive study of the dynamics of role conflict focused on the superintendents of Massachusetts public school districts (Gross, Mason, and McEachern 1958) have important implications for understanding the identity problem of pastoral caregivers. School superintendents have a complex role-set comprising teachers, taxpayers, administrators, community officials—and their conflicting expectations. School budgets, curriculum, classroom size, and maintenance and enlargement of school buildings are all battlegrounds for competing interests.

The Massachusetts school superintendent study established two social forces, sometimes working in concert, at other times working in opposition, that affected how a given superintendent resolved a particular role conflict. One force is the individual's

FIG. 6-1. The role-set of the hospital chaplain

sense of the *legitimacy* of the expectation. This is the moral dimension. For a superintendent to say, "I believe what the teachers want me to do on that issue is right," is to recognize the legitimacy of their expectation. The other force is the relative power of the groups in question. The researchers call this the *sanctions* dimension. Here the issue is what rewards and punishments will come to the individual for conformity to, or rejection of, the expectation. In contrast to the moral path, grounded in a sense of legitimacy, there is the expedient path, based on a sense of what positive or negative sanctions face the individual. Powerful partners have the capacity to impose *sanctions* in ways not possible for the less powerful.

The crucial dilemma of role conflict arises when Expectation A has the force of legitimacy while conflicting Expectation B has the force of sanctions. Four behaviors are possible when we face this dilemma. We can conform to Expectation A (the moral position), we can conform to Expectation B (the expedient position), we can perform some compromise behavior that represents an attempt to conform in part to both expectations, or we can attempt to avoid conformity to either expectation.

Waldo Burchard's study (1954) of United States Army chaplains demonstrates how pastoral caregivers resolve role conflict. Two conflicting values in American society clash head-on in the military chaplaincy: the separation of church and state, and the right of all citizens (including armed services personnel) to practice their religion. Burchard sought to determine how much conflict military chaplains experienced between their position as clergypersons representing religious denominations and their position as military officers representing the government and military establishment. Because major doctrines of Christian theology—love of enemies, universal brotherhood, peace, nonresistance to evil, and "thou shalt not kill"—hold a potential for conflict with military ideology, Burchard investigated the psychological mechanisms Army chaplains employ for resolving conflict.

Three mechanisms for resolving role conflict were most pronounced. First, most chaplains understood their primary identification as military officers, not clergypersons. That they had many nonreligious responsibilities such as leading the Character Guidance Program—instruction in what Burchard termed "godly patriotism"—fit more comfortably with this primary identification. Second, they employed rationalization for handling the ideological conflicts, for example, holding strongly to the "just war" theory and understanding the Sixth Commandment not as "thou shalt not kill," but as "thou shalt not murder." Third, there is evidence of compartmentalization, the tendency to see religious or moral values involved in their clergy work (for example, conducting religious services), but not in tasks that were governed by military regulations.

An American Civil Liberties Union study of army chaplains (Jonakeit 1973) details the ways the chaplaincy can be understood as an unconstitutional government establishment of religion.

Yet Burchard, who asked the question, "Is chaplaincy a state-established church?" found that 81 percent of the current chaplains and 54 percent of the former chaplains said no. That there is not more discomfort among military chaplains over the inherently conflictual position they occupy is explained by Burchard and others in terms of the selective process (self-selection and the military screening) that weeds out persons who have a prophetic or evangelical understanding of religion. Thus chaplains largely do not perceive role conflict because they recognize the military "system" as a given and exercise their religious leadership within its constraints (Vickers 1984).[2]

Returning now to the case of hospital chaplains, we need to consider how they resolve their role conflict. Physicians represent powerful persons in the chaplain's role-set. Hence their expectations have the force of sanctions. The expectations of others, however, often strike the chaplain with the force of moral legitimacy, pulling him or her toward a course in conflict with a physician's expectation. Thus the chaplain risks incurring negative sanctions for actions he or she believes are morally right. The following case illustrates the dynamics of such a role conflict situation for a chaplain.

James is a hemodialysis patient in his late fifties. Married very briefly in early adulthood, he now lives alone in a rustic mountain cabin. Kidney failure forced James, a carpenter by trade, to stop work. He exists on a subsistence government disability income. James has dialyzed at a hospital's dialysis unit for five years. He is considered by the hospital staff to be a noncompliant patient because of his failure to adhere consistently to the unit's strict dietary and fluid intake restrictions and his tendency to miss his scheduled dialysis "runs" when he feels unusual fatigue and depression.

One particular week, James had missed his three regular dialysis appointments on Monday, Wednesday, and Friday. On Saturday morning, the dialysis chaplain phoned James and discovered that he was extremely depressed, overcome with the problems of his subsistence life, and wanting to quit dialysis and die. The chaplain said he understood how James might feel that way but asserted that James ought to consider a decision as momentous as terminating dialysis only when he was his "normal self," not when he was in a deeply depressed mood and when his lucidity was affected by the uremic poisoning resulting from his missed dialysis treatments. Realizing that James was in serious need of a dialysis run, the chaplain offered to come, pick him up, and drive him to the hospital. James said he "might" consent to go.

The chaplain notified the charge nurse of the dialysis unit that he was driving to James's cabin and would probably persuade James to undergo a dialysis treatment. After further discussion at his home, James agreed to dialyze. In his weakened condition, James needed assistance in dressing and walking to the car. At the hospital, the chaplain seated James in the dialysis waiting area while he went into the treatment area to notify the staff that James had arrived. There he met one of the unit's supervising physicians who was reluctant to dialyze James on an unscheduled basis and on a day when the unit was unusually busy. Demanding a rationale for dialyzing James, the doctor asked angrily: "Chaplain, why are we doing this?" He replied, "Dr. ——, simply because it's right! When dialysis patients say they want to stop dialysis, we tell them not to make a hasty decision, and you yourself know how different staff members talk with them to make sure they are making a good decision. No one has talked to James about this, and he's not in any condition to make an intelligent decision right now anyway. We don't have a choice about dialyzing him."

The doctor authorized James's run. James required special treatment for some days but succeeded in getting through that crisis and moved on to more stable days. About a year later, James did die, but not from a decision to stop treatment.

James's case illustrates how role conflict arises for pastoral caregivers in the institutional context. What the dialysis chaplain did for James that Saturday falls in the category of the caregiver's "patient advocate" role. Because of organizational power structures, pastoral caregivers often clash with the powers-that-be in defense of the less powerful members of the system, whether they be lower-ranking staff or the organization's client population.

The incident involving James and his special dialysis run cannot be understood as a simple "good guys versus bad guys" morality play. A dialysis unit is a complex social organization. Patients on hemodialysis, one of several modes of dialysis, spend on average nine hours a week on dialysis machines. A major commitment is required of patients undergoing treatment for chronic kidney disease, as well as the commitment of their families and, of course, the hospital staff members who care for them. The "culture" of this particular dialysis unit was exemplary in a number of ways. Chronic illness and dependence on high-tech modes of treatment easily cause patients to feel a loss of control over their lives. This dialysis unit sought to maximize patients' sense of personal control. The staff encouraged patients to learn to set up their own machines and do their own "sticks," the insertion and removal of the needles. The values of the unit had the purpose of fostering patients' sense of ownership for their physical well-being. The rules rewarded responsible adult behavior and punished lack of discipline.

A cardinal rule related to keeping scheduled dialysis appointments. The personal requirements of each individual patient were taken very seriously when making the weekly schedule of patient "runs," but once patients had been assigned their regular times, they were expected to use personal discipline to be present. If a patient missed a dialysis appointment without a compelling reason, he or she was expected to wait for the next appointment, usually two days away (three over weekends). In an emergency situation, a patient could come to the emergency room and have a blood test. If the patient's blood potassium (a critical indicator of the need for dialysis) was above a certain level, then a special dialysis run would be authorized. In other words, the rules strongly encouraged compliance, but the staff would not let patients die if they failed to keep the rules.

Rule-making and rule-enforcement have unanticipated consequences. James's case is an example. He had no illusion about his lack of discipline. The rules were a mirror for him, whereby he judged himself the same way the staff judged him, as a noncompliant and therefore defective person. The chaplain had no idea why James missed his Monday and Wednesday appointments that week. By Friday and Saturday, however, his failure to "show" was based, the chaplain believed, on a self-judgment: "I'm not worthy to ask special favors from the dialysis staff, who, after all, have gone out of their way for me on many occasions." James knew about the "emergency procedure," but his feeling of worthlessness at the end of that week probably caused him to believe that he had no right to activate that process. In fact, on that Saturday morning, his potassium level might not have been quite high enough to meet the doctor's standard for an emergency run. If he came to the emergency room, would he "fail" the test? So rules that have the legitimate purpose of motivating patients to accept personal responsibility probably, in James's case, had the unanticipated consequence of "demotivating" him.

The rules also presupposed that patients would have family or friends who would exert influence to prevent them from committing passive suicide. James did not. His transportation situation was also problematic. The dialysis social worker devoted major attention to setting up transportation systems involving taxi services or volunteer drivers for the older, blind, or seriously disabled patients. James was still relatively self-sufficient and physically able and, being capable of still driving himself to the dialysis center, did not yet require those special transportation services. In short, the rules did not take account of special situations such as that of James.

The rules of the dialysis unit expressed its organizational culture. The pastoral caregiver ministering in an institutional setting must work in a "system" that has its own special rationale, but that may not take into account the particular difficulties of individual people. The "system" often seems heartless, although as in the case of this dialysis unit's supervising physicians, they were persons with compassion. Two conflicting definitions of the situation collide, causing the role conflict experienced by the pastoral caregiver.

Directors of Pastoral Care:
In the Middle of the Middle

If institutional pastors are men-and-women-in-the-middle (like industrial foremen, waitresses, police, and school superintendents), directors of pastoral care are still more in the middle, because their job requires balancing the demands of the organizational culture "from on high" and the needs of the chaplains for autonomy and identity as primarily religious personnel "from below."

My interviews in 1992 with ten directors of pastoral care departments in metropolitan St. Louis revealed the enormous institutional pressure on pastoral care departments in this day of cost-containment and DRG's (diagnosis-related groupings) and the creative ways in which directors are responding. The result is a high-wire balancing act, where directors couch the mission, program, and budget requests of their departments in terms of the operational goals of the larger hospital system. We get a good hint of the cost-benefit yardstick being applied to pastoral care budgets in the following remark by a hospital administrator:

> What's the rationale for having a Pastoral Care Department in this hospital? Why, an able chaplain can answer that question pretty quickly through a few hours of good work in our intensive care unit family waiting room. We have ICU patients hooked up to life-support systems costing this hospital thousands of dollars a day. If our chaplains can develop some rapport with those patients' families and help them come to terms with taking Mom or Dad off the machines sooner rather than later, they've justified their salaries right there, besides of course the other good things they do.

Pastoral care directors emphasize two institutional payoffs from effective pastoral services: (1) patients who receive an effective response to their spiritual needs in the crisis situation of hospitalization need less nursing care and have shorter average stays and (2) well-staffed pastoral care departments, through their contacts with pastors and others in the community, constitute important referral services for revenue-producing hospital programs.

Pastoral care departments treasure evidence that their pastoral services help the institutions financially. Several years ago, I worked closely with a heart bypass surgery patient and his family. He had complications and a longer than usual hospital stay. Two or three of us chaplains at one time or another worked with him, his wife, and his adult children. The wife remarked to me, when he was being wheeled out of the hospital to go home: "You know, chaplain, the money this hospital spends on your salaries is some of its best-spent money." I told her we especially appreciated hearing comments like hers because our director was continually forced to defend our department's budget. I wished that an administrator had been present to hear her remark!

Most of the St. Louis directors I interviewed understood one of their primary responsibilities was to keep their chaplain staff members healthy. Pastoral care, attracting compassionate and "giving" people, poses a high risk of burnout. However, unlike the parish, where there is no intermediary between the congregation and the pastors, in the institutional setting directors can interpose themselves in ways to prevent staff burnout.

The directors in a number of cases withstood pressures to fragment the solidarity of their departments. Hospital units were asking for designated chaplains whose salaries would be paid by those departments, not out of the pastoral care department budget. Very tempting, indeed, were these proposals, for their effect would be to reduce pressure on the pastoral care budgets. However, chaplains "owned" by the separate departments and relocating their offices to those departments meant they would become isolated from their colleague group and lose the benefit of the small religious community as their reference group. For the latter reason, some directors rejected what were tempting offers.

Strongly differentiated pastoral identity poses particular challenges to directors of pastoral care, for they must often defend the actions of their chaplains to the administrators when there is "flak." When controversy arises, directors can choose to side with the administration or with the chaplain involved in the incident. It is striking how often directors support their personnel against institutional pressures toward conformity.

To recapitulate the discussion, we have so far looked at role conflict as often posing a dilemma between expectations with the force of moral legitimacy and expectations having the force of sanctions. The case study of James and his dialysis treatment pointed up the caregiver's resolution of role conflict, in a complex situation of competing definitions of the situation, on the side of moral legitimacy. Then we looked at directors of pastoral care and how they stand under intense pressure to balance the institutional demands of hospital administrations and the requirements of good pastoral care. In the last section of this chapter, further attention is focused on how caregivers resolve their role conflict in accordance with the pastoral and not the medical worldview. However, in the next section, we need to give attention to the collective struggle in the pastoral care community to resolve this conflict between worldviews, the controversy over the "professionalization" of pastoral care.

Professionalization and Formation:
A Pastoral Dilemma

Pastoral caregivers, through their training in clinical pastoral education and participation in the pastoral associations, have been exposed to the "big debate," and its terms echo in their consciousness as they work in institutional settings. The controversy over the professionalization of pastoral care is illuminated by sociological analysis in terms of role conflict. In recent years, pastoral care has increasingly assumed the form of a modern profession with the emergence of national professional societies, promulgation of standards, accreditation of training programs, and certification of pastoral caregivers. The professionalization movement has stirred criticism, not over the effort to ensure good quality pastoral care, but over the way these developments seem to contribute to its secularization.[3]

Professionalization, as we saw in chapter 4, is the process by which an occupation defines a body of knowledge as its special area of expertise, develops standards for admission to the occupational circle of credentialed or licensed members of the profession, and sets up structures for maintaining self-government and discipline. In addition to the established professions of medicine and law, many other occupations claim "professional" status and have already won, or are in the process of seeking, state and national recognition: engineers, architects, psychologists, social workers, counselors, and physical and occupational therapists.

Sociologists, as we saw earlier, have sharply different perspectives regarding professionalization. The functionalist tradition focuses on the special contribution of the professions to modern society, based on their commitment to knowledge, maintenance of high standards of service delivery, and collectivity-orientation (in contrast to self-orientation). The conflict tradition understands professionalization as a process of occupational control for the purpose of increasing the power and autonomy of an occupational group and also of guaranteeing the scarcity of the service through monopolizing the gatekeeper function, thus protecting its economic status.

Those in pastoral care who have advocated greater professionalization have used the functionalist argument. They stress the importance of standards of competence for pastoral caregivers as a protection for employing organizations and individual clients. Facing the alternative of outsiders (administrators, personnel departments, hiring committees) who have little understanding of pastoral care making uninformed decisions to employ caregivers, the professional pastoral care associations, through the certification process, make the evaluation of caregivers' skills according to standards based on the collective wisdom of the pastoral community itself. The emphasis on standards of competence for pastoral caregivers is shared by all four of the major pastoral care associations in the United States: the American Association of Pastoral Counselors (AAPC), the College of Chaplains (largely Protestant), the National Association of Catholic Chaplains, and the Association for Clinical Pastoral Education (ACPE).

The controversy in pastoral care over professionalization concerns the nature of those standards. The same role conflict we see confronting caregivers working "between worlds" is writ large in the collective conflict over the legitimate reference group for pastoral standards. The pastoral care community is in the middle between the expectations of more secular professional groups on the one side and the expectations of the more theologically oriented religious communities on the other.

The professional role-partner groups exerting influence on the pastoral care community—primarily psychiatrists, other physicians, psychologists, and social workers—expect that pastoral care will endorse standards that meet their secular canons of validity. The problem is that pastoral care is a religious activity and therefore its special body of knowledge is, to a significant degree, religious knowledge. Religion in the modern society is highly pluralistic. According to secular standards, religion does not qualify as public truth (as medical science or legal knowledge do) but only as private belief. According to this understanding, the religious content of pastoral care should not be made part of its professional standards. Under this constraint, pastoral care is limited to the promulgation of standards relating only to pastoral *method* and to the body of knowledge that qualifies as good science, namely, psychological knowledge. Yielding to these secular expectations, pastoral care becomes a distinct profession in form but not content.

Influences from the other direction, the religious community, pull pastoral care toward a more theological identity. Central to these expectations is the assertion that religious knowledge has the character of public truth. The intellectual defense of this position, drawing on modern philosophical ethics and on the sociology of knowledge, is skillfully articulated by Lesslie Newbigin in *The Gospel in a Pluralist Society* (1989).[4] Pastoral care in this view is a search for truth, for adequate definitions of the careseeker's situation. Truth is understood here both as personal truth and as universal truth. The former search is what Alastair Campbell, Scottish pastoral ethics professor, in his book, *Professionalism and Pastoral Care* (1985, 73–74), understands when he says that pastoral care expresses "a love that seeks truth, while yet [being] conscious of the dangers of a judgmentalism that can impede that search." Karl Barth had the latter search in mind when he would ask a student in his class, after Barth had made a profound theological assertion, "Herr Schmidt, is that true?" Asked in all seriousness and humility, Barth's question signified this great theologian's belief that absolute truth exists but that he could claim no infallibility in grasping it. Pastoral care oriented to this view of religion as a search for public truth would ideally engage in dialogue about definitions of the situation with the same seriousness and humility as Barth (but, as we saw in chapter 5, with more attention to subjective experience than Barth was willing to give).

Four implications of these theologically oriented expectations for pastoral care are significant. First, there is a heightened recognition of the importance of tradition as a resource for pastoral care. Tradition here means both the biblical and church traditions. James D. Whitehead and Evelyn Eaton Whitehead (1980) in their model of reflection in ministry stress the interaction of Christian tradition, personal experience, and cultural information as the three key resources in pastoral care. The "professional" training model represented in clinical pastoral education (CPE) has neglected the use of scripture in pastoral care. Walter Brueggemann, the biblical scholar, addresses this neglect and asserts that the biblical scriptures are "living human documents" (Anton Boisen's classic phrase) just as much as the lives of patients and clients. Brueggemann holds that many CPE supervisors undertook their theological training in a day when scripture was understood as flat and static, whereas the newer view sees biblical texts as dynamic and alive (25th Anniversary Videotape, ACPE, 1992). Some CPE supervisors, among them Brueggemann's colleague Brian Childs, are taking his criticism seriously and building the use of scripture into the worship, study, and patient care phases of their programs.

Second, this viewpoint challenges pastoral care to resist the cultural hegemony of modernist thought, Rieff's "triumph of the therapeutic." Alastair Campbell believes clinical pastoral education exemplifies the cultural captivity of professionalized pastoral care:

> [CPE] tends to freeze pastoral care in the images of human need and distress created by contemporary depth psychology, without providing the means for demythologizing the current world view, exposing its cultural and historical relativity and its inadequate imagery. (1985, 81)

To resist secularizing influences, Campbell urges pastoral care to sustain the sociology of knowledge perspective toward modern culture outlined in this book's chapter 2.

Third, the theological critique of the "professional" model stresses the need for *formation* of the pastoral caregiver. Formation is a concept with strong roots in the Roman Catholic tradition referring to the preparation of future priests in Christian spirituality. Again, Campbell writes:

> "Formation" entails not merely the acquisition of knowledge or the fostering of skills, but also the development of character. It suggests that a state of being must precede any action, any doing. It implies a holistic approach to those undergoing preparation, one that deals with their emotions, attitudes, and value commitments, so far as these relate to the knowledge and skills required for pastoral care. (1985, 79–80)

Campbell believes the professional model for training pastoral caregivers fails to provide a "formation" experience, partly due to the separation of theological study and clinical experience, the one achieved in the seminary, the other in the CPE course or pastoral counseling clinic. Hauerwas (1981), Duffy (1983), and Mudge and Poling (1987) all emphasize "formation" models of Christian life, pastoral care, and caregiver training.

Fourth, from the theologically oriented point of view, the locus of pastoral care is the congregation, not the one-to-one relationship between caregiver and careseeker. As Campbell indicates, this issue was the prime concern of British pastoral caregivers who resisted professionalization. A leader of the British pastoral care movement, physician and theologian R. A. Lambourne, opposed the formation of a national pastoral counseling organization in Britain comparable to the American Association of Pastoral Counselors. Lambourne's basic idea (1963) was that pastoral care needed to stress the congregational aspect of lay care and that the primary function of "experts" (full-time pastoral care specialists) was to train the laity. Another British pastoral care leader, Frank

Lake, a missionary doctor who became a psychiatrist, also placed heavy emphasis on the congregational context of care. A neo-Freudian heavily influenced by object relations theory, Lake staked out a psychologically reasoned argument in his major text, *Clinical Theology* (1987) [1966], that separation anxiety is healed in the church context where pastoral counseling is coupled with sacramental Christian worship.

Thus using the perspective of role conflict to illuminate the controversy over professionalization, we see the pastoral care community being tugged from opposite directions in its identity struggle. Newly published histories of the American Association of Pastoral Counselors (Van Wagner 1992) and the clinical pastoral education movement (Hall 1992) document the organizational dynamics of this struggle. Observation of recent developments yields conflicting evidence about the resolution of the struggle as we look to the future.

Primary identification with the "professional" expectations was seen at a recent ACPE annual meeting, where a CPE supervisor in a southern state described a problem he faced operating a clinical pastoral education program partly funded by the United Methodist conference. He reported that some members of a church board were questioning continued funding of his program because ACPE guidelines insisted that programs be nondiscriminatory in terms of sexual orientation. These board members objected to gay and lesbian persons being trained for church leadership, which was in conflict with denominational policy. The other CPE leaders attending this particular workshop seemed automatically to reject the church board's objection as homophobic, prejudiced, and ultraconservative. There appeared to be no empathy for the wrenching dilemma facing the churches over the issue of ordaining gay and lesbian ministerial candidates. That leaders of a national pastoral care organization do not identify with the anguished personal struggle many broadminded church leaders experience over the homosexual ordination issue suggests that many clinical pastoral educators use the professional or secular liberal community, rather than the religious denominational communities, as their primary reference group. At the least, the ACPE incident seemed to be a manifestation of the weak organizational ties between the church denominations and the CPE movement.

There are signs of change, however, in this movement's orientation, toward greater identification with the "religious" perspective. Interest grows in parish-based clinical pastoral education, or as George Fitzgerald (1993) prefers to call it, "supervised congregational ministries." Full-time pastoral care specialists are reestablishing connections with congregations and church judicatories, as is evidenced in chaplains becoming moderators of presbyteries and conferences. Conversations with clinical education supervisors reveal concern about a perceived former neglect of theological reflection and serious efforts to buttress this dimension of the training experience. There is also the increasing use of scripture, which has already been mentioned.

Thus just as the individual caregiver must constantly resolve role conflict between the religious counselor and the humanistic professional, the pastoral care communities' struggle over "professional" and "religious" identity will continue. The evidence cited above, however, suggests that after a considerable period when the "professional" model has held strong appeal, there is often a movement toward the "religious" model of a more differentiated pastoral care.

The Differentiation of Pastoral Identity

The move in recent years toward differentiation of pastoral identity around *theological* diagnosis has been immensely positive. Much credit for this development goes to Paul Pruyser (1976) who sounded the challenge to pastoral caregivers to embrace the basic resources of their calling. Ministers and theological students who came to the Menninger Clinic for clinical pastoral training seemed "at sea" regarding their distinctive role.

> They did not quite trust their parishioners' occasional use of theological language and their presentation of theological conflicts. Issues of faith were quickly "pulled" into issues of marital role behavior, adolescent protest against parents, or dynamics of transference in the counseling situation. There seemed to be an implicit suspicion of the relevance of theology, both to any client's life and to the method and content of the pastor's counseling process. (Pruyser 1976, 28)

The theological diagnosis advocated so strongly by Pruyser in *The Minister as Diagnostician* will be discussed and illustrated in chapter 7, where we call it "pastoral assessment." Many institutional pastoral caregivers have available an important vehicle for differentiating their pastoral identity, namely, their documentation of pastoral assessments and pastoral plans in patient medical records ("charts") and their oral communication of these assessments to other members of the treatment staff.

Differentiated pastoral identity can be articulated wherever pastoral caregivers interact with other staff involved in the treatment process or leadership situation. Community leader meetings, interdisciplinary staff meetings, hospital case conferences, mental health boards, and school board meetings are examples of situations that challenge caregivers not to soft-pedal the religious exploration involved in pastoral care. For example, at the weekly staff meeting of a hospital unit, attention was focused on Dennis, a young male patient whose progress seemed unusually slow. Drinking heavily, he was involved in a late-night one-car accident, which left him a paraplegic. Dennis had expressed strong anger to the unit chaplain over having survived the accident. "I wanted to die," he had asserted. The chaplain's turn came to make his assessment of Dennis's situation. Rather bluntly, the chaplain said, "The assumption seems to be present among us here that our treatment goal for Dennis is to return him as closely as possible to his status before the accident. That is an inadequate goal for this patient. Dennis felt his life, at the time of his accident, was meaningless. He is angry with the paramedics and everyone who pulled him through. We *must* deal with Dennis's system of life-meaning. Otherwise we may make him physically mobile but leave him in spiritual despair." A physician then commented, "Well, Dennis has the example of all you highly motivated staff as role models. That should rub off on him." The chaplain replied, "That's not enough." The chaplain continued his conversations with Dennis about his anger and about his choices regarding life-meaning. Gradually Dennis established a direction for his life and put his talents to work for the disabled community. As the chaplain's earlier remarks at the hospital staff meeting reveal, pastoral caregivers define their role through the questions they ask and the goals they assert regarding careseekers' situations.

Staff coalitions are another critical aspect of pastoral role definition. Some nonpastoral staff of any institution (in the hospital case, for example, doctors, nurses, housekeepers, attendants, custodians) are religious believers. Those whose religious identity is most salient for them personally are frequently members of conservative churches. Pastoral caregivers are often ambivalent toward forming coalitions with the conservative religious staff, because the pastoral staff are often more liberal and because they do not want to be "typed" as religious fanatics through these associations. Their unease in relating to these religious staff members reflects, more than anything, unresolved issues regarding their own religiosity. Religiously committed staff are a valuable source of pastoral referrals, and too often the pastoral staff alienate these potential referring agents by their disdainful attitude.

An attitude that "only professionals can do things right" pervades modern institutions. This mentality militates against the effective use of volunteers and laypersons in the care process (Haugk 1984). Pastoral care is a prime example of a discipline that cannot limit expertise to only ordained or CPE-trained or otherwise "qualified" caregivers. The "professionalization" of pastoral care sometimes creates this wrong impression. The Holy Spirit is the source of deep Christian caring, not a clinical training course or a university graduate degree in counseling. I want to be very clear here. I am not advocating the deployment of well-meaning but unscreened and untrained volunteers in responsible pastoral care positions. Which is our reference group when we consider whether to use competent volunteers in our pastoral care departments? Is it other professionals or is it the religious community? Some of the most exciting pastoral care in hospitals is done by trained volunteers. Professionals dare not forget this fact.

Differentiated occupational identity is communicated visually through distinctive dress. We see this in uniforms and "fashion." Pastoral care departments have different conventions about pastoral attire. A widespread tendency, especially in large hospitals, is to wear medical uniforms (such as white lab coats). Other institutions ask male Protestant chaplains to wear coat-and-tie (with pastoral care staff badges) to signal the difference between the Catholic and Protestant chaplains. This latter practice causes much confusion between chaplains and physicians.

PATIENT: Oh, you must be Dr. McIntyre, the specialist my doctor told me would be coming by. [*Looks expectant.*]

CHAPLAIN: No, I'm Rev. Jones, one of the hospital chaplains. I realize that you're a new patient."
PATIENT: [*Looks disappointed.*] Oh, I see, what can I do for *you*?

Clerical garb (such as clerical collars) is the clearest means of unambiguous definition as religious personnel. Some Catholic
priests occasionally lament their clerical attire, saying it puts an
obstacle in the way to rapport. I disagree. Simple clerical garb
states clearly the religious dimension of interaction. Many parish
pastors whose denominations do not require clerical attire find, as
I did in an urban neighborhood, that such a "uniform" works
wonders in outreach work. Seminary field education students assigned to a large public hospital discovered how clerical shirts
helped them define a pastoral identity. Whatever the pastoral context, the issue of dress needs to be considered in terms of reference
groups. With which reference group do I identify? Which group is
it important that I do *not* look like? The issue of dress is contro-
versial, and my colleagues do not all agree with me on this question. My belief is that pastoral caregivers' primary identification is
with the religious community, not the medical staff. Differentiating their dress from the latter is important, where possible, to facilitate a *pastoral* definition of the care situation.

Such externals as dress and staff coalitions are outward expres-
sions of pastoral caregivers' consciousness. As the sociology of
knowledge approach to pastoral care asserts, that consciousness—
the religious worldview—depends upon a plausibility structure
that gives it reality-maintenance. Pastoral care, wherever it operates but especially in the institutional context where it confronts
secular and alien organizational cultures, must give special attention to the construction of a strong religious plausibility structure.
Otherwise pastoral caregivers are constantly at risk of cooptation
into the secular power structure and the secular worldview.

If worldview requires ethos, then pastoral caregivers depend
upon religious ritual and devotional activity on a continuous basis
for reality-maintenance. A Lutheran missionary nurse, working
with Mother Teresa in her Calcutta orphanage, tells how the
nurses, in the midst of their agonizing work with dying children,
went to the chapel as often as every half-hour for prayer. She asserted that only constant reinfusion of the divine energy could sustain the staff against despair. This worship had the vital function of

reality-maintenance for the nurses' religious worldview, just as worship does in the institutional settings where many pastoral caregivers serve. Pastoral care departments in most Catholic and Episcopal institutions have the special advantage of a daily liturgy. Other institutions have worship less frequently. A pastoral staff needs to understand worship and the sacraments as being vital *for them*, not just as a religious service offered to the institution and its clients. Communions done in patient rooms are not just a pastoral service, but a reality-maintenance structure for the pastoral caregivers. Pastoral staffs must seek creative ways to prevent their worship experience from becoming routinized and unmeaningful and to assure its centrality as an affirmation of the transcendent reality in their midst.

Caregivers' private devotional life undergirds their ministry together as well. Pastors, chaplains, and counselors—busy with long hours of administration, counseling, and crisis-intervention—are at risk of neglecting personal prayer and scripture study. Continual reference to this danger is made in the pastoral manuals on spirituality (Holmes 1982; Thayer 1985). Like corporate worship, the devotional life is at risk of neglect through loss of its vitality. Pastoral caregivers are discovering innovative modes of prayer and study that renew their excitement over "practicing the presence of God."

Conclusion

This chapter has focused on the problem of pastoral identity in institutional settings. The concept of role conflict oriented the discussion, showing how pastoral caregivers work in organizational cultures that emphasize secular goals. The power structure of large organizations works to co-opt institutional pastors into those goals. Pastoral care resolves its role conflict, and successfully differentiates its distinctive role in the larger system, by stressing the *legitimacy* of its religious perspective. This is often done by appeal to the general mission statement of the institution or to the religious principles of the larger society.

To sustain pastoral identity as caregivers especially equipped for exploring with careseekers the possibility and implications of religious definitions of their situation, pastoral caregivers must create plausibility structures that keep them oriented to the religious worldview. This means giving major attention to daily rituals—corporate and private—for reality-maintenance. Otherwise, pastoral care is continually subverted by the dominant secular worldview.

There are no easy answers to the dilemmas posed for pastoral identity in the modern institutional context. The thrust of this book is to challenge pastoral caregivers to assume riskier and more conflictual identity. I believe that a major source of burnout among pastoral caregivers—parish pastors and institutional chaplains alike—is the emotional damage caused by repeated submission to subtle institutional pressure. But I must alert the reader to the risks of the more prophetic and religious pastoral stance: pastoral caregivers do not have a strong power base in institutions, despite the high legitimacy of their roles. In terms of the cost-benefit equation, we are expendable. In defining the pastoral role, we are engaging in critical choice-making. Being "humanistic professionals" wins for us solidarity with many physicians, administrators and other powerful staff, but making this choice has deep religious and emotional costs. Yet our employment status is obviously in jeopardy when we stress the religious perspective of our vocation. No decision about pastoral identity made at one particular time settles the issue for long, because our resolve is tested anew almost daily. To put this in Bonhoeffer's terms, What is the cost of discipleship? Turned the other way, What is the cost of compromise?

7. Pastoral Care as Social Process

This final chapter addresses the applicability of the sociological perspective to the practice of pastoral care. How is the caregiver who has developed C. Wright Mills's "sociological imagination" better equipped to do real-world pastoral care? Theories are great, but pastoral caregivers are practical people who expect a payoff in the quality of their caring, counseling, and supporting of hurting, searching modern persons.

The focus of this chapter is an experienced hospital chaplain, The Reverend Jeanne Adams, and her pastoral care of a dialysis patient, Susan Collins. We will see how Rev. Adams integrates sociology, psychology, and theology to form a holistic perspective that orients her interaction with Mrs. Collins and guides her pastoral strategy.

Pastoral care is portrayed in this chapter as an emergent social process involving a caregiver and a careseeker engaged in dialogue exploring alternative definitions of the latter's life situation. The energizing dynamic of this dialogue is the careseeker's struggle to construct an adequate worldview, a definition of her life situation that best handles the disparate sensory impressions, meanings, emotions, and expectations that she encounters. We will see how religious definitions of the situation, positing transcendent spiritual reality, generate ambivalent reactions in a modern careseeker like Susan Collins. Religious definitions are not only attractive for their capacity to integrate empirical and nonempirical reality but also repulsive, because of their conflict with modern culture. Like most pastoral situations, this careseeker's crisis is complex, requiring that the struggle for a more adequate perspective be waged on a number of fronts and over a considerable period of time.

Pastoral care as an emergent social process can be represented by a simple five-stage model depicted in figure 7-1. In the first stage, *defining pastoral identity*, pastoral caregivers create a set of expectations among potential careseekers and institutional coworkers about the perspective and goals of pastoral care. In the second stage, *pastoral assessment*, the caregiver listens carefully as the careseeker explains the problem. This may, of course, be a careseeker group such as a family or work group. The caregiver "processes" this listening to the careseeker's present definition of the situation, juxtaposing in his or her mind a religious definition that constitutes a provisional theological diagnosis. The third stage, *formulation of a pastoral plan*, involves determining a strategy for work with the careseeker or group that will be discussed with the individuals involved and revised as seems appropriate. In the fourth stage, *pastoral interventions*, the pastoral plan is implemented through interactions with the careseeker and significant others. Central to these interventions is dialogue exploring alternative definitions of the evolving situation. The last stage, pastoral evaluation, represents the caregiver's intentional reflection about the outcome of the pastoral process.

As the diagram indicates, there are feedback effects in this system. The interventions generate new information that cause revision of the initial pastoral assessment. Provisional evaluation takes place constantly, leading to modification of the pastoral plan.

This model of the pastoral care process is based on a system for pastoral documentation used in many Catholic hospitals. This is known as the APIE system from its key aspects: assessment, plan, interventions, and evaluation. My model adds an initial stage, defining pastoral identity. Hospital chaplains use the APIE system as an outline for documentation of pastoral care in patients' med-

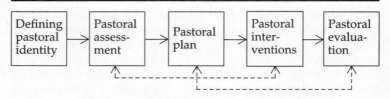

FIG. 7-1. Stages of the pastoral care process

ical records. The virtue of this model is its clear recognition of the need for theological diagnosis as a basis for care, of the value of a clear strategy of treatment (discussed under most circumstances with the careseekers), and of the benefit from focused reflection about the outcomes of care—how the strategy worked.

This five-stage model, although developed in the hospital context, has general applicability to other pastoral contexts. Pastors who have attended hospital workshops where the APIE model is discussed comment on how it helps them understand the process of their pastoral counseling. The model makes explicit what tends in much parish pastoral care to be diffuse and somewhat vague. Specialized pastoral counselors engage in these same steps, with pastoral assessment being a critical factor.

Defining Pastoral Identity

The pastoral care process is significantly influenced by the way in which caregivers define their pastoral role. As we saw in chapter 6, caregivers face critical choices regarding their identity. To understand Jeanne Adams's pastoral care of Susan Collins, we must look briefly at the institutional context of her work and at her role identity.

Jeanne Adams works as a staff chaplain in a large regional hospital, a position she has held for five years. Among her unit assignments, she is the chaplain for a dialysis unit similar to the one where James, the "noncompliant" patient discussed in the last chapter, dialyzed. Her kidney unit cares for approximately 100 patients on hemodialysis who receive two or three treatments per week of approximately three and one-half hours duration and 150 patients on continuous ambulatory peritoneal dialysis (CAPD), whose self-administered treatments at home are supervised by the dialysis unit staff. Due to the different shifts of hemodialysis patients, some starting as early as 7 A.M. and others finishing at 9 P.M., Chaplain Adams varies the timing of her rounds through the unit in order to make periodic contact with most of the patients. She normally spends from one-half hour to two hours per day in this unit.

The organizational culture of this hospital unit must be understood in contrast to its "competition," the for-profit kidney centers in the metropolitan area. The staff take pride in working as a "health care team" where "high tech" is coupled with "high touch." This corporate identity is important, for the staff believe they provide better care and more personal attention to the patients than the commercial centers.

The staff of this hospital unit is made up of four nephrologists (M.D. kidney specialists), about twenty-five nurses, several technicians, a full-time medical social worker, and other auxiliary personnel such as dieticians and respiratory care technicians who, like the chaplain, serve as primary specialists in dialysis but work in other units. The medical social worker has primary responsibility for the psychosocial evaluation and support of the dialysis patients. When the primary chaplain is not available, other members of the hospital's department of pastoral care provide pastoral services.

As the dialysis chaplain, Rev. Adams has achieved a relatively high degree of differentiated identity as a religious counselor. Her identity-formation has evolved over the three-year period she has been assigned to dialysis. She has met regularly with the medical social worker and the charge nurses, discussing the physical, emotional, social, and spiritual situation of the patients. Although none of the physicians has a notable appreciation for religion, Rev. Adams has gained their respect as an assertive and compassionate staff member able to look at the "big picture" of holistic care. She no longer feels tense around the medical social worker, who seemed to fear usurpation of her psychosocial role. The two work closely together, the social worker bringing her expertise as a specialist on the social situation of kidney patients and the chaplain offering hers as a skillful counselor around life-meaning issues. At first, the unit's staff made special referrals to the chaplain only of patients who were known to be especially religious. As time went on, however, she received more referrals of nonreligious patients and their family members who staff members felt could profit from her skills in "value clarification." Two specific responsibilities the chaplain assumed were informing patients about the deaths of their co-patients and conducting funerals for a number of patients. Often nurses and occasionally physicians attended these services.

Rev. Adams had an early conversation with Susan Collins when she first started dialysis. At that time she learned that Mrs. Collins, age sixty-two, was a long-time insulin-dependent diabetic whose progressive kidney disease had reached the point where her physicians insisted she start hemodialysis. A surgeon had inserted a

Gortex graft, known as a fistula, under the skin of her left arm, through which the needles ("sticks") of her hemodialysis treatments would be inserted. Asked about her family, Susan told Rev. Adams about her husband Ed, who had retired two years earlier as a foreman in a large manufacturing plant; about her three adult children, all married; and about her four grandchildren. Mrs. Collins said she and Ed were on the membership rolls of a Protestant church in their town of 3,000, located fifteen miles from the hospital, but she admitted they had been inactive for a number of years. In this initial conversation, Susan Collins struck the chaplain as an outgoing, motherly woman, frightened of what the future held for her as a person with what the doctors ominously referred to as end-stage renal failure. Through the next months, Rev. Adams spoke with Mrs. Collins probably once a week, the conversations dealing largely with the practical issues of adjustment to her demanding "job" of dialysis.

Pastoral Assessment

Seven months into dialysis Jeanne Adams had a significant pastoral conversation with Susan Collins. This encounter served as the basis for a pastoral assessment by the chaplain and for her formulation of a pastoral plan to respond to Mrs. Collins's crisis. We will review this conversation presently. First, however, we need to discuss the broad dimensions of pastoral assessment. In the previous chapter, we considered the value of pastoral assessment and theological diagnosis as important aspects of the differentiation of pastoral identity. Pastoral assessment is a creative process of analysis and synthesis that yields a religious definition of the careseeker's situation. For the dialogue of caregiver and careseeker, the pastoral assessment becomes a working option as an alternative definition of the situation.

Pastoral assessment starts with the caregiver carefully eliciting the careseeker's definition of his or her situation: "Tell me how things are going." "How do you see the problem?" "You told me you are worried about something. Tell me about that." All the skills of active listening, paraphrasing, and encouraging elaboration are involved here: "How does that make you feel?" "Let me make sure I understand—when Alice says that to you, you really hear her saying . . ." "Tell me more about that." By this process of elaboration and expansion, the caregiver invites the careseeker to communicate the larger perspective that is his or her basis for interpreting the immediate problem.

Pastoral assessment involves formulating a provisional theological diagnosis of the careseeker's situation based on her or his disclosure of spiritual, emotional, psychological, and social information. The Catholic APIE method focuses on four basic questions for pastoral assessment:

1. What is the patient's understanding of God or of a higher power?
2. How does the patient perceive the meaning of his or her illness or present situation?
3. What social support system does the patient have?
4. What is the source of hope for the patient?

Due perhaps to the very simplicity of these four questions, they prove remarkably durable in use by caregivers doing frequent pastoral assessments.

Now we return to the case and watch how Rev. Adams made her pastoral assessment of Susan Collins's crisis. Doing her rounds among the patients this particular morning, the chaplain stops by Mrs. Collins as she sits in a blue recliner chair next to a quietly humming dialysis machine. Susan tells her she feels unusually depressed today.

PATIENT: I'm not my usual "upbeat" self these days.
CHAPLAIN: How come?
PATIENT: I'm tired *all the time*. All I do at home is sit in a chair. I make lunch. That's all I have the strength to do. Ed does all the rest.
CHAPLAIN: You feel down because you can't be active like you were before you became ill?
PATIENT: Yes. I'm worthless. I can't make any contribution. My husband even has to help me get dressed. I'm a leech, a parasite. I cry a lot. I'm only half alive.
CHAPLAIN: You sound frustrated that you have to depend on Ed and your family for so much help?
PATIENT: That's very true. I *used* to be so independent. Ed *tells me* that he doesn't mind doing the cooking and housework. I know he loves me, but I feel so unworthy of his love.

CHAPLAIN: It sounds like you might question whether Ed is really as accepting of the situation as he says. Is that right?

PATIENT: Sometimes. I know he looked forward to his retirement when we planned to travel and he intended to do a lot of fishing. We took one trip to Mexico and then I got sick. He rarely goes fishing because he worries about me so much. And he's a man, and men assume that cooking, shopping, and housework are "woman's work."

CHAPLAIN: These ideas about men's roles and women's roles are changing these days with women working. It's not so cut and dried now as maybe it was.

PATIENT: That's just it. I worked part-time for three years but I didn't contribute much income. The rest of the time I was a full-time homemaker.

CHAPLAIN: Do you ever feel any anger toward Ed because he's well and able to do all these things around the house and you're sick and really very restricted?

PATIENT: I hate to admit it but I do. It's very unfair that I feel that way because he's not to blame for me being sick. That's just the way things worked out.

CHAPLAIN: Do you sometimes get angry with God?

PATIENT: Do you mean about having kidney failure?

CHAPLAIN: Yes.

PATIENT: Well, that's hard to say. We're not supposed to be angry with God. And God isn't supposed to give us more than we can bear.

CHAPLAIN: You don't quite know what that means?

PATIENT: Right.

The alarm on Mrs. Collins's dialysis machine sounds, indicating her treatment is completed. Her nurse comes to disconnect her tubing and needles.

CHAPLAIN: I see that it's time for your nurse to take you off the machine. I see you reading some while you're here for your treatments. I have a little book which I loan to patients called *May I Hate God*? It's by a Catholic priest named Pierre Wolff. He says it's important that we tell God honestly how we feel toward God. Otherwise we bury the anger and it comes out in indirect ways like depression. Would you be interested in looking at it?

PATIENT: I'm not doing as much reading as I used to. My eyes aren't so good, but yes, I'd like to look at it.

CHAPLAIN: I'd better go along. I'd like to talk with you some more about the issues we've been discussing. Would you like to do that some other day during your run?
PATIENT: Yes, I really would.
CHAPLAIN: OK. We'll plan on doing it.

This conversation served as the basis for the chaplain's pastoral assessment. Rev. Adams notes several sociological dimensions of the conversation. The theme of *self-worth* dominates Mrs. Collins's remarks: "I'm worthless." "I'm a parasite." These self-evaluations result from her image of an idealized self, herself earlier in the prime of health, and her contrast of that image in her present condition. She has what Goffman calls a spoiled identity. By using able-bodied people like her husband as her reference group, she experiences a sense of severe relative deprivation.

Coupled with the self-worth issue is the problem of *power*. Susan Collins feels little autonomy or independence. Control has been taken out of her hands. She feels totally regulated by the schedule of her dialysis treatments and by her sharply restricted physical energy. Like the situation in complex modern societies, where the locus of power is so diffuse and amorphous as to be unidentifiable, the "system," who or what is responsible for her powerlessness, is very unclear to her. "That's just the way it worked out," she says.

Restricted *communication* characterizes the patient's social system. Notice that she articulates her own definition of the situation (spoiled identity, lack of autonomy) but she also presents her husband's definition of the situation as she perceives it. Here is a striking aspect of the "social self," the fact that we base our social identity not on the real attitudes of significant others toward us but only on the cues they emit. Mrs. Collins suspects that her husband may be engaging in some "impression-management," sounding more accepting of the household situation and her illness than he really is. She is ambivalent about knowing what his real feelings are, but she does wonder. She withholds communication of her true feelings, judging her anger both toward Ed and toward God improper and thus inexpressible.

The opposite of restricted communication is full and honest communication. What possibilities exist in this situation for achieving such communication? Rev. Adams realizes this issue ought to be raised in subsequent conversation. Susan's feeling of the illegitimacy of expressing her anger appears to create a sense of isolation. It also seems to be a component in her sense of powerlessness. Socializing the difficulty, to use Boisen's term, would help overcome her sense of isolation. Expressing her real feelings, however, threatens her self-image as a fair-minded person appreciative of the help her husband (and God) give her and, more basic, seems to her to jeopardize the continued supply of that necessary assistance.

Gender issues are intricately intertwined with her sense of low self-worth and powerlessness. Susan Collins associates self-worth and gainful employment. Bringing home a paycheck, which she did for only a brief period, is what makes one a first-class person. Homemaker and mother are less worthy endeavors, and thus women are expected to "work" their whole lives while men can expect to "retire." The value system of the larger American society reinforces the equation of gainful employment, maleness, and human worth. This conversation does not go into the issue of sexuality, but Rev. Adams understands that a frequent source of depression of chronically ill women also relates to their feeling that they are "depriving" their husbands of sexual satisfaction.

There may be a subtle power issue between Ed and Susan Collins over his fishing. Susan says he rarely goes fishing—one of his favorite activities—because he worries about her. Worry can be a covert form of control. The worrying partner, who will not leave his or her spouse because some terrible thing might happen, creates an expectation that such an unfortunate event will happen and denies the spouse freedom to be as self-sufficient and risk-taking as possible. *If I can't leave you because something terrible might happen to you, then you feel no freedom to do things that might endanger you.* This is as true of the disabled adult as it is of the overprotected child. The fears of both husband and wife need to be expressed and dealt with. Otherwise, Mrs. Collins will continue to feel that her illness is preventing her husband from having an anticipated pleasure of his retirement years, and she will feel guilty about this. As a practical help, the chaplain thinks of Lifeline, the tiny radio transmitters carried by infirm persons that activate their telephones and a help network. What a valuable source of security this technology is for both the patient and concerned family members!

A psychological dynamic in the situation is evidenced in the conversation. The patient expresses particular disgust for the fact that her husband has to help her get dressed. The memory of childhood dependency and powerlessness is triggered by adult disability.

The chaplain's sociological approach to pastoral assessment traces the attitudes of individuals to societal values. She realizes that the American value system of "instrumental activism" is mirrored in Susan Collins's perspective. A person's value is measured in terms of his or her productivity. That she cannot perform her accustomed social roles makes her not a person and not a woman. Her self-characterization as a "parasite" conjures up the image of American attitudes toward welfare-dependent persons. This emphasis on occupation, activity, social roles, and "doing" imposes terrible strains on the elderly and ill that, together with the youth culture of physical fitness and beauty, rob them of a sense of vital societal involvement.

Jeanne Adams senses that her patient's theology is not a source of strength or meaning. Earlier, as we saw, the chaplain had learned that this patient and her husband are nominal Protestant church members. The present conversation did not explore the area of religion extensively, but the chaplain did hear that the patient believes we owe God love, that anger is improper, and that she feels shortchanged by God; her need is greater than God's supply. Susan Collins's God sounds distant and impersonal.

This theology, in fact, has a strong ring of alienating religion, religion that has been shaped by the value-system of the society rather than the other way round. We saw in chapter 5 how the routinization of religious vision takes out the transcendent fire. For Mrs. Collins, God may be American ideology writ large: "productive people" equals "good people"; illness is equivalent to deviance; and God's love is conditional.

Pastoral assessment that expresses the sociological imagination understands the careseeker's definition of the situation, as we have sketched some of Susan Collins's major themes and some of the chaplain's provisional reflections, to be a choice among alternative definitions. The pastoral assessment is a theological diagnosis, the construction of a religious definition of the careseeker's situation that pursues greater adequacy and integration. The assessment involves standing outside the careseeker's cognitive world and examining its reality-assumptions.

As she engages in theological reflection on Susan Collins's worldview, Rev. Adams realizes that the Christian religious vision turns Mrs. Collins's worldview upside down. Susan now has the strong people on top and the weak and ill people on the bottom; Jesus' worldview, with its "upside-down kingdom"[1] and a crucified God, upsets the worldly power system. Rev. Adams asks herself, Can I articulate a religious definition of Mrs. Collins's situation that might serve as a viable alternative both to her worldview and to her accompanying self-image as a dialysis-dependent, always tired, worthless, and parasitic woman?

These reflections served as the basis for Chaplain Adams's pastoral assessment of Susan Collins and her current crisis. Five issues appear paramount:

1. Communication with her husband and with God seems impaired due to Mrs. Collins's feeling that anger must be warranted to justify its expression.
2. Her lack of autonomy and sense of control creates a feeling of powerlessness, which may be exacerbated by her husband's worry and overconcern.
3. Gender issues of "women's role" and feelings of inferiority for not having been gainfully employed contribute to her low self-esteem and depression. Pastoral involvement should explore her possible feelings of being insufficiently appreciated as a good homemaker and mother.
4. From being outgoing and "upbeat," Susan Collins seems now to be introspective, negative, and unable to see any positive contribution she can make to others. Feeling so depressed and victimized by her illness, she cannot think of her alienation and self-pity as essentially sin—brokenness in her relationship to a God who loves her, wills wholeness for her, and needs her despite her infirm physical condition.
5. The patient's worldview appears to reflect the reality assumptions of alienating religion, a religious viewpoint captive to modern American culture. An alternative worldview, a more transcendent and de-alienating Christianity, posits an upside-down kingdom that is "good news" for the poor and infirm.

Chaplain Adams wrote a brief summary of her pastoral assessment in the patient's medical record. She realized that three of the four assessment questions are addressed: the careseeker's sense of God, the meaning of the illness, and the social support system. The source of hope was not yet addressed. It is important to note that the pastoral assessment is tentative and provisional, based on fragments of information. On the basis of his or her experience, the pastoral caregiver forms some hypotheses for exploration in the subsequent encounters.

A Pastoral Plan

On the basis of her assessment, Rev. Adams develops a pastoral plan to address the significant issues of her conversation with Susan Collins. Before looking at the specifics of this plan, we need to say a word about what a pastoral plan is from a social psychological point of view.

The social self of the pastoral caregiver, like that of the careseeker, has the "Me" and "I" phases we examined in chapter 3. Careseekers express expectations toward the caregiver regarding the help they want. Pastoral assessment takes into account how the careseeker understands the role of pastor, pastoral counselor, or chaplain. The social identity of the caregiver, his or her "Me," gains expression in the pastoral assessment.

The pastoral plan, the strategy of response to the careseeker, expresses the "I" phase of the caregiver's social self, his or her personal identity. Considering the complex of expectations, what considered set of initiatives will the caregiver set in motion?

The chaplain's pastoral plan for dialogue with Susan Collins had two ready-made ingredients. First, she needed to remember to bring the book with her the next time the patient would be dialyzing. She could make a few remarks about Pierre Wolff's small book, which praises the Hebrew attitude toward God—"Yahweh, you are a so-and-so for letting things get so bad, and you'd better come to my aid quickly here, or I'm a goner." Second, the first meeting of a new dialysis support group was scheduled for the following week, and she wanted to make a special appeal to Mrs. Collins to attend. Previous experience with Alcoholics Anonymous and a cancer support group had convinced Rev. Adams of the reference group value of persons sharing a common situation engaging in direct and honest conversation.

Three other ingredients of the chaplain's plan touched on points in the pastoral assessment. First, there was the communication problem between Susan and Ed Collins. Both partners seemed to fear honest communication. Illness imposes severe strains on marital relationships, and the Collinses seemed to be playing a very safe game around expression of negative feeling, thus causing both to feel isolated. To address the communication issue, the chaplain believed it was necessary for her to see both Susan and Ed together. She would explore the issue initially with Mrs. Collins and then try to set up a meeting with them together. A special area of the dialysis unit, the isolation room, was a good place for the chaplain to counsel with individuals or families in private.

Second, the chaplain figured that Mrs. Collins needed some vehicle to be a caregiver rather than constantly be the care-receiver. If she could realize that some people depended on *her*, this would counteract her extreme feeling of personal worthlessness. This would best be outside the family, with persons whose need was clear but whose situation would not overwhelm this physically and emotionally depleted woman. How this might be accomplished would require some investigation.

Third, and probably most important, the chaplain wanted to explore with Susan Collins the assumptions undergirding her apparent theology of God's conditional love. She desired to juxtapose an alternative religious definition of the situation for the two of them to explore together. The pastoral caregiver realized that some parabolic way of contrasting the two worldviews would be helpful—not a philosophical or abstract discussion—since Mrs. Collins, although an evidently literate person of good intelligence, did not seem like the scholarly type.

Implementing these different strategies would take some time, but the chaplain realized that the patient would be coming to dialysis regularly and thus opportunities would be present over a period of time to work on these issues. She appended to the summary she wrote of her pastoral assessment in the patient's medical record notation of the patient's permission for her to explore further the issues and of her tentative plan, stressing the support group and a possible meeting with both Ed and Susan Collins.

Interventions

Unlike the occasional and casual encounters caregiver and careseeker might have in the normal course of their common life, as in a congregational parish setting or in a passing meeting in the hospital dialysis center, interventions are intentional encounters that relate to the issues of the pastoral assessment and plan. A series of interventions took place over a period of time with Susan Collins.

The first intervention came two days later when the chaplain remembered to bring along Wolff's book, *May I Hate God?* when she did her dialysis rounds. Mrs. Collins was feeling ill during her treatment that day, so the chaplain said only a few words about the book and left it with her.

Some days passed before the chaplain saw her again. This time the focus of conversation was the upcoming meeting of the new dialysis support group. Mrs. Collins was feeling less "down" than on the day when she and Rev. Adams had talked about her depression. The chaplain gave her a little "pep talk" about the value of support groups ("people who share a common problem talk about how they feel; everyone seems to be helped by this sharing"). Susan was worried that she would "have to talk"; the chaplain laughed and said, "No, it's all very informal and voluntary. People only share if they feel like it." Susan was tentative about attending, saying she never knew from one day to the next how she would feel.

Rev. Adams was glad to see Susan present at the dialysis support group meeting. Seven patients, two of their spouses, and three staff members (medical social worker, a charge nurse, and the chaplain) attended this first meeting. Each of the staff made informal statements about how they understood the experience of dialysis from the point of view of their discipline. The social worker talked about the patient and his or her family; the nurse dealt with medical aspects; and the chaplain spoke about spiritual considerations. As it turned out, something the chaplain said had significant meaning for Susan. Rev. Adams said:

> From a spiritual point of view, chronic illness poses unusual problems for people in American society. This society's culture stresses activism, productivity, doing this and that. Our self-identity is horribly tied up with our work and careers. We answer

the question, Who are you? by naming our occupation. The effect of the high value placed on work and activity is to create a very difficult situation for unemployed people and for persons with chronic illness. From a spiritual point of view, and here I speak from the Christian perspective, our personal worth does not depend on our productivity or the many roles we play or how good our performances are. Our basic worth resides in our being, not our doing. We are created in the image of God and our basic identity has its central anchorage in that fact. Our personal worth is therefore just as great when we are ill as when we are healthy.

The patients were relatively quiet at this first "icebreaker" meeting and mainly asked questions of the staff members.

The chaplain's next intervention came the following week, when Susan talked for the first time about her ambivalence concerning religion. That particular day the patient was dialyzing in a quiet alcove of the dialysis center away from the main nursing activity, and she was in a particularly reflective mood. Susan remarked that the chaplain's point at the support group about human worth coming from our "being" and not our "doing" had struck her as very helpful. After they discussed how social values shape our self-image, Rev. Adams asked Susan to tell her about God. The patient seemed to welcome this question, for she talked freely about going to Sunday school as a child, attending church revival meetings as a teenager, and getting married in the church. As she grew older, her image of God split into the good God and the bad God, the one loving and the other rejecting. She spoke about her progressive withdrawal from church and her loss of interest in religion. At the close of this reflective conversation, Mrs. Collins said that the crisis of her illness was causing her to think again about the issue of religious faith but that she had very conflicting feelings. The chaplain had to stop at this point due to a meeting; the two agreed to continue the conversation at a later time.

Rev. Adams's two-week vacation occurred at this point, so the next time she spoke with Susan, there had been two more meetings of the dialysis support group. The patient had now attended three meetings and was eager to report how valuable she found them, especially the sharing among the dialysis patients themselves. "Around my family, I always feel so ill and useless. But I'm realizing when we dialysis patients talk among ourselves, we *all* feel this way. It's like this is 'normal' for us. So we don't have to apologize all the time and feel guilty that *this is the way it is*." Rev. Adams recognized in what Mrs. Collins was telling her that the patient was experiencing a salutary change in her reference group. The chaplain felt encouraged by this fact, for she believed this change in orientation would help her patient develop a better self-image.

The next week Ed happened to be sitting with Susan when the chaplain was doing rounds. The chaplain had met Ed a number of times when he was bringing his wife up for her treatments. Rev. Adams pulled up a chair and talked with the couple together. It was not the most private location, but the unit was so noisy that day no individual conversation could be heard from afar. The chaplain remarked to Ed about his interest in fishing. Susan got into the exchange, telling Ed she felt very uncomfortable for preventing him from doing something he enjoyed so much. In fact, she spoke very forcefully to her husband, saying she thought he worried about her too much and that she felt more confident about being alone at the house, now that she had become more accustomed to the dialysis process. Ed seemed to detect signs of his wife's former independence. His reaction was, "Maybe I should think about getting together with Jim [a friend] more often like we used to."

It was several weeks later that Rev. Adams and Susan had a chance to continue their earlier conversation about theology. In her pastoral assessment, the chaplain had sensed the need to use a parable of some kind to contrast Mrs. Collins's worldview, where she felt so worthless and God seemed so distant, and the upside-down kingdom of a more authentic Christian vision. Chaplain Adams realized she wanted the patient to hear a twofold message. On the one hand, from the Christian standpoint, our self-esteem is based on our "being" as God's children, not our "doing," and on the other hand, there is special work for disabled and shut-in people to do. This particular day the conversation had returned to religious issues, and as Rev. Adams reacted to Susan's further questions about her usefulness, she used the metaphor of "fanner bee Christians" (Glenn Clark 1932).

CHAPLAIN: Have you ever heard of fanner bees?
PATIENT: No.
CHAPLAIN: You know how bees have social organization with a division of labor: the queen, the workers, the drones. Well,

there are bees called the "fanner bees." Their job is to stay inside the hive, beat their wings, and create a draft of air that forces the bad air out one side of the hive and draws fresh air in the other. Well, this author, Dr. Glenn Clark, talks about "fanner bee" Christians. He held the spiritual power of prayer to be a vital necessity for our country and our world, and he believed the people who could best do the kind of praying that is needed are shut-in folk who can't be out running around. They have enough inner peace and serenity to accept and do this vital work of drawing the fresh air of the Spirit into our land.

PATIENT: It's interesting you raise the issue of prayer, because that's been on my mind lately. I often feel this "presence" around me. I can't explain it to Ed, he's such a rationalist. It's like we're surrounded by this unseen spiritual realm. When I was a child, my mother always told me to pray to God when I had a problem. This kidney failure is the biggest problem I've ever had, and I've been trying to pray but then I think, prayer is just wishful thinking.

CHAPLAIN: I think the problem a lot of people have about prayer is they try to pray only alone. That way they get overwhelmed with doubts about what they're doing. I urge people to join a prayer group. Prayer in a small group of committed Christian people has enormous power. You get the same feeling of sharing and unity that you are experiencing in the dialysis support group. Often it's hard to really believe in the reality of God when we're lying awake at night beset by our fears, but in a prayer group that sense of spiritual presence you spoke about is experienced as very real.

Susan Collins seemed to find this observation interesting, but she could not see any guidance in it for herself, because her physical condition had cut her off from people and groups, "the world out there," as she put it.

The next morning Chaplain Adams called the pastor of the church where the Collinses were inactive members. She identified herself as the dialysis chaplain, said she was working with Susan Collins, and asked if the church had an active women's prayer group meeting for prayer and study. When the pastor reported that the congregation did not currently have such a group, Rev.

Adams briefly reviewed her pastoral assessment of Mrs. Collins, stated that locating a prayer group where she might refer her care-seeker for spiritual care was part of her pastoral plan, and explained that she intended to consult other churches in the area in her search for such a group. The second congregation she called held a Wednesday night prayer meeting but did not have small prayer groups. The third church she called did have prayer groups. The pastor reported that their most active group was a women's prayer and study group meeting on Tuesday mornings. The chaplain explained that Mrs. Collins was an inactive member of the other church but might be interested in this prayer group if one of the women would be willing to provide transportation. The pastor gave the chaplain the phone number of the group leader. The time of this group's meeting was fortunate, the chaplain realized, because it would not conflict with Mrs. Collins's dialysis scheduled on Mondays, Wednesdays, and Fridays.

The next time the chaplain saw Susan, she told her about her inquiries and about the women's prayer group at a church in her town. It turned out Susan knew the woman whose name the pastor gave as its leader. Rev. Adams asked her if she might like to attend. Her response was equivocal. She said her conversations with Rev. Adams had rekindled some long-dormant religious thoughts, but she expressed hesitancy because she didn't know if the women would understand about her illness and she hated to impose even more on Ed or one of her women friends for transportation. The chaplain asked, "Do you want to call the woman and talk about it? It might not be a problem for one of them to swing by and get you." The experience of the dialysis support group was having a positive effect on Mrs. Collins, so she was beginning to see new possibilities for her life "in the world." "Yes, I will call her," Mrs. Collins agreed.

Despite some apprehension, Susan Collins made the contact with June Smith, the prayer group leader, who warmly encouraged her to come to the group, explained the group was small (eight) but very loyal, and said she would be glad to provide transportation herself. Mrs. Collins said she was worried that she would feel uncomfortable and asked if she would have to pray aloud. The leader said, "Oh, we all feared that when we started. No, you don't have to do anything until you feel absolutely ready." Sufficiently convinced, Susan Collins said she'd like to try it, arrangements were made for picking her up, and she attended. It turned out she knew a couple of the other women also, and much to her surprise, she felt very much at home in the group.

This small group of women, committed to the Christian spiritual journey, had a transforming effect on Susan Collins. The chaplain saw the changes from month to month in her attitudes about God, about Ed and her family, and about the possibilities of her life. Within the constraints of her chronic illness, she found herself living with new energy and a more positive outlook.

The chaplain recalled how one of the points of her pastoral assessment concerned Susan Collins's introspective and negative attitude, how she could not see any positive contribution she could make. One day she reported that she and Ed had "adopted" a very elderly man and his wife, neighbors, as the special object of their care. "They're special people who we didn't know very well until recently. They really depend on us. I go over nearly every day for at least a few minutes. Ed helps the gentleman do some work around the house. I just sit and talk, especially with her. I can really identify now with older people who feel helpless and confused."

Rev. Adams also noted how Mrs. Collins began to think about the societal implications of her discoveries. "How do you change the values of a society?" she asked. "We don't value the contribution of our elderly people and those of us who have chronic illness." The chaplain replied, "Now we're talking about politics!" Rev. Adams couldn't help feeling amazement at how far Susan Collins had come from her personal crisis of fear and depression to her present broadening human perspective.

In short, the chaplain's initial interventions set in motion a series of developments for this dialysis patient that changed her life from dependency and depression to some independence and a much more positive outlook.

Pastoral Evaluation

The sociological approach to pastoral care focuses particular attention on the outcomes of the care process. Only by reflecting on what we do is it possible to increase the effectiveness of pastoral care.

Chaplain Adams reviewed her initial pastoral assessment and

sought to evaluate the process of her care of Susan Collins. Her
early theological diagnosis made when the patient hit a crisis
point dealt with five issues: (1) The patient's worldview seemed
inadequate to deal in a positive way with her situation, since it
conceived of people as strong or weak, and as a woman with
chronic illness, she had no basis for self-esteem. A religious worldview, the chaplain realized, could turn that world upside down.
(2) The patient appeared to have a communication problem with
Ed and her family, particularly related to the expression of anger.
(3) She had lost virtually all sense of control, which seemed to be
exacerbated by Ed's worry. (4) There were gender issues related to
her sense of "women's role." (5) The assessment raised a theological consideration that the patient's sense of being the victim of her
disease obstructed the realization that her alienation toward God
was sin.

The pastoral plan involved a strategy to reorient the patient's
reference group orientation (the support group); a strategy to
change the sense of low control (meeting with Susan and Ed); and
a larger strategy of counseling to propose an alternative worldview that would address Mrs. Collins's theology and her self-
identity within that theology.

The objectives were accomplished to a significant degree partly
through the chaplain's interventions but also through the successful impact of the two group experiences, the dialysis support
group and the church women's prayer group. The transformation
in the patient's attitudes exemplifies the sociological axiom that
group contexts have greater power for facilitating attitudinal
change than do individual counseling contexts. Of course, this is
not an either/or proposition, for both the group and the individual situations have their particular values.

Evaluation includes reflection on the ethics of the caregivers'
strategies. A question could be raised about Chaplain Adams's
process of searching for a prayer group for Susan Collins. Although the caregiver explained her rationale for this search to the
careseeker's nominal pastor, she did not make an effort to solidify
the Collinses' affiliation with their church. As it turned out, Susan
Collins was being offered a religious involvement in a different
denomination, which could conceivably lead to a transfer of membership. The chaplain felt this venture into the ecumenical community was worth the risk, because of her firm belief in small

groups as the incubators of religious consciousness. Some persons might question the ethics of her action.

In summary, this case study of the pastoral encounters between Rev. Jeanne Adams and Mrs. Susan Collins illustrates how the stages of pastoral care—identity-formation, assessment, plan, interventions, and evaluation—create an emergent social process structuring the interaction of caregiver and careseeker. A particular focus of this case was how Chaplain Adams integrated the perspectives of sociology, theology, and psychology to generate a unified pastoral care that attends to the three points of the triangle: self, God, and the society.

Pastoral Care and Sociology: Toward Greater Integration

We come to the end of a journey through sociological theory in search of perspectives useful for contemporary pastoral care. The end of a journey deserves a fitting commemoration. My two contexts—the academic and the pastoral—suggest different appropriate endings, for courses end with a final examination and pastoral care ends with a party! So perhaps the instrumental and the expressive tasks can be merged here as we retrace our steps.

The sociology of knowledge informed our whole journey. This perspective subjects to scrutiny the taken-for-granted reality assumptions of modern people. For pastoral caregivers there is cause for joy in the "sociological imagination," for it demonstrates that people's worldviews are a choice among alternatives. It is liberating for people to realize that they have choices and options. Pastoral care is portrayed as a vehicle for the careseeker's choice-making. A key to resolution of the careseeker's problem is locating it within the larger context of reality assumptions. As a religious counselor, the pastoral caregiver has special skills for articulating the possibility and implications of religious viewpoints. In the pastoral dialogue, the religious definition of the situation becomes a viable option of choice for the careseeker.

Religion leads a precarious existence in modern society because of the absence of a plausibility structure that provides reality maintenance for it. My image was a hot-air balloon that needed a functioning burner to stay aloft. A key aspect of the secularization of modern societies is the destruction of religion's plausibility structure. As we saw in the case of Allen, the cardiac patient, his religious experiences were delegitimized in his largely secular social experience. An adequate worldview for this troubled man needed to be big enough to handle both his perceptions of spiritual reality and his appreciation of science. The plausibility structures for worldviews in modern societies are not the total set of social rituals but rather the social interactions of a particular circle of people, the individual's reference group. Careseekers' perceptions are anchored in their reference groups. Therefore, attitudinal change for careseekers necessarily involves changes in their reference groups. This was illustrated in the case of Susan Collins when she began to use the viewpoint of her dialysis support group as the basis of her self-identity. She was no longer such an abnormal person. Her case also demonstrated the operation of plausibility structures. Religious consciousness depends significantly on having a religious community as a reference group, which she found in a women's prayer group.

Power and conflicts of interest pervade social relationships. Ideologies express and legitimate the social interests of dominant power groups in a society. Pastoral care, along with family systems therapy and secular psychological counseling, has often given insufficient attention to the power factor in relationships. Gender stratification—the relative power of men and women—is a key dimension of modern counseling and must not be obscured by caregivers' desire to achieve harmony and "peace" between individuals experiencing conflict. Goffman's pithy statement cited in chapter 4—"Gender, not religion, is the opiate of the masses"—points up the "power gain" of men in traditional interaction with women. Pastoral care sensitive to this issue traces the dynamics of gender power and powerlessness. Empowerment is a central pastoral goal, both in the small group contexts of marriage, family, and work group, and also in the larger society, through facilitating careseekers' participation in "mediating structures," voluntary associations and politically oriented groups working for societal change.

Pastoral caregivers want to promote healthy religion, and they confront a difficult issue when careseekers manifest unhealthy religion. We gave attention to religion that embodied prejudice, authoritarianism, and hierarchical views of the social order. This was called alienating religion, or religion under cultural captivity. The pastoral care process can facilitate careseekers' growth into broader perspectives that liberate the religious vision from its cultural package.

Organizational cultures of the institutions where many pastoral caregivers work exert strong pressures on their pastoral identity. These pressures create a situation of role conflict for chaplains and other institutional caregivers. Holst's phrase, "living between worlds," aptly characterizes the position of the caregiver working in health care, the penal system, the academic world, the military, and corporate industry. We looked at the risks involved for pastoral caregivers to assert a more differentiated identity as religious counselors, for this stance pits chaplains and other caregivers against the organizational power structures. The sociology of knowledge perspective was reapplied here in the emphasis on pastoral care departments forming an intentional community with corporate religious ritual and theological reflection, thus sustaining a plausibility structure for their identity as religious counselors rather than humanistic professionals.

The sociological perspective was then integrated with the perspectives of psychology and theology—viewpoints that are more familiar to pastoral caregivers—to form a unified picture as we took a more detailed look at one pastoral case. Five stages of pastoral care were portrayed there as an emergent social process: differentiation of identity, pastoral assessment, development of a pastoral plan, a series of interventions, and evaluation of the outcomes. The prime consideration through the pastoral care process is exploration of the careseeker's choices regarding definitions of his or her situation. Susan Collins assembled a set of cognitive elements to create a different worldview, one that was significantly informed by religion, and to shape a new self-identity.

Pastoral care today is experiencing a time of severe testing. Changes and upheaval in the larger society impact pastoral care in very obvious and in quite subtle ways. This book has argued, in short, that the sociological perspective is a significant resource for clarifying the major issues confronting pastoral care in the nineties. Sociology may not make the choices any easier, but it illuminates the options.

Appendix:
Biographical Notes

BELLAH, ROBERT N.   Bellah is best known as senior author of the popular book, *Habits of the Heart* (1985). Born in 1927, he was raised in Los Angeles. His religious roots are Presbyterian on both parents' sides. A sociologist trained at Harvard University, where his doctorate was awarded jointly by the Departments of Social Relations and Far Eastern Languages, Bellah did extensive studies of historic Japan in his early career (1957). Talcott Parsons was a formative influence on Bellah's thought. The strength of Bellah's social analysis comes in significant degree from his comparative approach to culture. In recent years Bellah has become a strong advocate of transcendent religion; his personal bent is toward sacramental Episcopalianism. Bellah is the Ford Professor of Sociology and Comparative Studies at the University of California. See his autobiographical introduction in Bellah (1970).

BERGER, PETER L.   Berger is known for his work in the sociology of knowledge and the sociology of religion. Born in Vienna in 1929, Berger emigrated to the United States at age seventeen, completed his undergraduate education in New York City, attended a Lutheran theological seminary for one year, then pursued a doctorate in sociology at the New School for Social Research in New York City. There he came under the influence of Alfred Schutz and sociological phenomenology. Berger has taught at the Hartford Seminary Foundation, Brooklyn College, Rutgers University, and in recent years, Boston University. His introductory sociology text, *Invitation to Sociology* (1963), is one of the all-time best-selling sociology books. Berger's approach to the sociology of religion in his early career—"methodological atheism"—changed in more recent years to a much more theologically oriented perspective. Berger's wife, Brigitte, is also a sociologist and is currently chair of the

Boston University Sociology Department. See Hunter and Ainlay (1986) for essays assessing Berger's sociological perspective.

BOISEN, ANTON T. Born in 1876, Boisen graduated from the University of Indiana, taught high school, and pursued studies in forestry before entering Union Theological Seminary in New York as a Presbyterian ministerial candidate. There he was especially influenced by George Albert Coe, a professor of Christian education who was a follower of John Dewey and George Herbert Mead. After graduating from Union, Boisen did sociological studies of rural church communities and had brief rural pastorates. Following hospitalization for mental illness, Boisen prepared himself to be a psychiatric hospital chaplain. As a chaplain at Worcester State Hospital in Massachusetts and adjunct faculty member in social ethics at Chicago Theological Seminary, Boisen was a founder of the clinical pastoral training movement. Boisen died in 1965.

DURKHEIM, ÉMILE. Durkheim was a father of modern sociology. The son of a Jewish rabbi, Durkheim was born in the French province of Lorraine in 1858. He attended the prestigious École Normale Supérieure in Paris. He taught philosophy, education, and sociology at the University of Bordeaux and then became a full professor of social science at the Sorbonne (University of Paris). The late nineteenth century was a period of intense anti-Semitism in France, evidenced in the famous Dreyfus case. As an adult, Durkheim was a religious agnostic who believed that modern societies needed a secular equivalent of religion to support moral integration. Durkheim was a pioneer in the use of comparative social data for building social theory, most strikingly demonstrated in his classic study, *Suicide* (1951 [1897]). Durkheim died in 1917, a man in deep grief over the death of his beloved son in the war. For an excellent biographical study of Durkheim, see Lukes (1973).

ENGELS, FRIEDRICH. Always subordinated to the towering figure of his colleague Karl Marx, Engels is now recognized as the more profound sociological thinker of the two, whereas Marx was the economist and political revolutionary. Born in 1820, the son of a wealthy German textile manufacturer, Engels went to Manchester, England, in 1842 to take a position at a factory partly owned by his father. He met Marx in Paris in 1844, and their lifelong collaboration began. Engels died in 1895.

GOFFMAN, ERVING.　Goffman introduced a distinctive perspective into sociology involving intense scrutiny of routine social rituals. He is best known for his first book, *The Presentation of Self in Everyday Life* (1959). Born in Canada in 1922, Goffman received his graduate degrees at the University of Chicago. A student of American anthropologist W. Lloyd Warner, Goffman used an anthropological approach with roots in Durkheim for studying modern societies. Goffman was a professor of sociology at the University of California. He died in 1982.

HUSSERL, EDMUND.　Husserl was a mathematician and philosopher who founded the phenomenological movement. Born in 1859, he was a professor at the Universities of Göttingen and Freiburg. Husserl's influence on modern theology is felt through Martin Heidegger, Hans Georg Gadamer, David Tracy, and Edmund Farley. His influence on phenomenological sociology moved through Alfred Schutz. Husserl died in 1938.

MARX, KARL.　Marx and Engels had a profound impact on European social thought in the nineteenth century. Marx was born in the Rhineland city of Trier in 1818, the son of parents descended from long lines of Jewish rabbis. He studied at the University of Berlin, which then exuded the spirit of the towering philosopher Hegel, and became one of the Young Hegelians. Leaving Germany because of its reactionary political temper, Marx went to Paris where he became a radical socialist and where he met Friedrich Engels. Commissioned in 1847 by a group in London called the Communist League to write a manifesto, Marx and Engels produced the famous *Communist Manifesto* in 1848. Marx spent years working in the British Museum on the volumes of his *Capital*. Marx died in 1883. See L. Coser (1971) and Collins (1985) for excellent treatments of the working relationship between Marx and Engels, two very different personalities.

MEAD, GEORGE HERBERT.　Mead was the pioneer of the symbolic interactionist perspective in sociology. Born in 1863 in Massachusetts, Mead grew up in Oberlin, Ohio, where his father was professor of homiletics at Oberlin College. Mead's mother later became president of Mt. Holyoke College. Mead studied at Harvard, the University of Leipzig, and the University of Berlin. His interests were philosophy and physiological psychology. A friend of

John Dewey's, Mead joined Dewey as part of the philosophy department at the University of Chicago when that institution opened in 1892. Mead taught in that department until his death in 1931. Mead was not a stirring teacher, but a small group of students recognized the brilliance of his understanding of social psychology. His major book, *Mind, Self, and Society*, was assembled for publication from the shorthand notes taken by students. The four great American pragmatic philosophers are generally recognized to be Charles Peirce, William James, John Dewey, and George Herbert Mead. See L. Coser (1971) for a good overview of Mead's life and thought; also see the new biography by Gary A. Cook (1993).

MERTON, ROBERT K. Merton, born in 1910, is a leader (still active but somewhat emeritus) of the functionalist school of sociology. Unlike his teacher at Harvard, Talcott Parsons, who did grand social theory, Merton focused on "theories of the middle range." Merton developed some of the key structural concepts in sociology such as role-set and role conflict and extended the theory of reference groups. A long-time professor at Columbia University, Merton is especially well known as a sociologist of science (chemistry, physics, biology).

PARSONS, TALCOTT. Parsons was the most renowned American sociologist through the 1950s and 1960s. Born in Colorado Springs in 1902, where his father was a Congregational homeland missionary, Parsons earned his bachelor's degree at Amherst. He then went to England and Germany in the early 1930s, studying at the London School of Economics and the University of Heidelberg. He earned his doctorate in economics at Harvard. Parsons's blockbuster study, *The Structure of Social Action* (1937), introduced the thought of Durkheim, Weber, and Italian social thinker Vilfredo Pareto to the American sociological community, which until then had been little influenced by European sociology. From his position in the Harvard economics department, Parsons in 1950 was named the first chairperson of the university's new Department of Social Relations, which united in one department the fields of sociology, cultural anthropology, and social psychology. Parsons became the leading spokesperson for the functionalist school of sociology. A prolific writer, he explored virtually every subfield in the sociological gamut. He brought a religious zeal to his sociological work, focused on building a social systems foundation for the moral integration of

American and modern Western society. Thus he translated the religious perspective of his father's strong Social Gospel message into a secular vision, building the kingdom on earth. See Buxton (1985) for the study most interesting to theologians of Parsons's intellectual and religious perspective. Parsons died in 1979.

SCHUTZ, ALFRED.　Schutz made a major contribution to sociology through joining the philosophical phenomenology of German mathematician and philosopher Edmund Husserl and the sociology of Max Weber. Born in Vienna in 1899, Schutz came to the United States from Germany as an émigré scholar in the 1930s. With other European intellectuals who had fled Nazi Germany, Schutz taught sociology at New York's New School for Social Research. He exerted a major influence on Peter Berger's thought. Schutz died in 1959.

TOCQUEVILLE, ALEXIS DE.　He was a French aristocrat who exerted a powerful formative influence on European and American political sociology. Born in 1805, Tocqueville traveled to the United States during Andrew Jackson's presidency and later wrote his two-volume comparative study of French and American government, *Democracy in America* (1835). Tocqueville's theory of mediating structures informs the sociology of David Riesman (1950), Robert Bellah et al. (1985), and Berger and Neuhaus (1977). Tocqueville died in 1859.

WEBER, MAX.　Weber was a towering nineteenth-century German intellectual figure who more than any other social scientist shaped the understanding of the dynamics of modern industrial societies. Born in 1864 in Erfurt, Weber grew up in Berlin, where his father was a member of the German Reichstag. The Weber household was a meeting place for the intelligentsia of Berlin. Weber suffered his whole life from psychic torment related to the psychological dynamics of his family, as his father was a worldly and secular liberal, and his mother, a devout and pietistic Calvinist. Weber's consciousness reflected the ambivalence toward religion these cross-pressures generated. Possessed of a mind of encyclopedic scope, Weber conducted studies of economics, sociology, political science, comparative religion, and music. Weber was a professor at the University of Heidelberg. He died in 1920. See Bendix (1960) for a good intellectual portrait of this important early sociologist.

Notes

1. Sociology for Pastoral Care

1. Two good sources for exploring the interface between theology and sociology are Martin, Mills, and Pickering (1980) and Perkins (1987).

2. Browning finds the humanistic psychologists holding a principle of near utopian harmony of all individual interests, needs, and desires. "In this literature there is the remarkable implication that, when all people are fully aware of their own organismic needs and completely attuned to their own valuing processes, an almost preestablished harmony of wants and desires will reign over society and conflict will be at a minimum if it does not altogether disappear" (1987, 68–69).

2. The Sociology of Knowledge and Pastoral Care

1. For an excellent introduction to the issues posed by the sociology of knowledge for clergy and other religious workers, see the essays in Hargrove (1984).

2. See Augsburger (1986) for a thorough study of pastoral care in cross-cultural situations.

3. Bredemeier and Stephenson (1962, 2) offer this quotation from Walter Lippmann. A search through some of Lippmann's writings does not reveal the exact source. A close equivalent is found in his *Public Opinion* (1922), 81.

4. This chapter concentrates on one tradition of the sociology of knowledge, the phenomenological tradition associated with Edmund Husserl, Max Scheler, and Alfred Schutz. In chapters 4 and 5 major attention will be given to the Marxian tradition of the sociology of knowledge, which was given strong expression by Karl Mannheim (1936).

5. The analysis here follows Clifford Geertz's reconceptualization (1966) of Schutz's multiple levels of reality (1962).

6. The phenomenological approach to the sociology of knowledge informs the theology of Edward Farley. See his *Ecclesial Man* (1975) and "Phenomenology and Pastoral Care" (1977).

7. Daniel Bell, in his book *The Cultural Contradictions of Capitalism* (1976), develops an important theory of the disjunction of the technoeconomic realm, the political realm, and the "culture" in modern Western societies. See my discussion of this book in Furniss (1992). Bell understands the social psychological consequences of this disjunction in a way similar to Parsons and Berger.

8. Berger in his latest book uses a hard-to-translate German word to describe people's experience of another reality breaking into their "normal" world: *Doppelbödigkeit*. "[This term] derives, I think, from the theatre, and refers to a structure, such as a stage that has more than one floor; those who walk about on the upper floor may at any moment fall through a trapdoor onto the lower one" (1992, 129). Berger discusses in some detail the novels of a German novelist, Robert Musil, who gives sustained attention to reality as doppelbödig.

3. The Individual, Community, and Society in Pastoral Care

1. For an excellent discussion of Freud's formulation of the social self and of Freud's sociology in general, see Bocock (1976), esp. chap. 3.

2. Boisen's autobiography is very relevant in understanding his idea of socializing difficulty and evil. As a college student, Boisen was troubled by sexual fantasies and psychically induced orgasms. He reports the feeling of liberation when he got up the courage to talk with others about his sexual compulsions (Boisen 1961, 47).

3. The members of the Orthodox Jewish synagogue described in sociologist Samuel Heilman's participant-observation study (1976) illustrate the "exclusivist" strategy. In this case study of a religious organization, the author demonstrates skillful use of the symbolic interactionist perspective of George Herbert Mead, Herbert Blumer, and Erving Goffman.

4. Power, Inequality, and Empowerment in Pastoral Care

1. LIFO Training, an acronym for Life Orientation Training, identifies four personal orientations toward leadership and group process: Supporting/Giving, Conserving/Holding, Controlling/Taking, and Adapting/Dealing. The course developers hold that groups need the expression of all four orientations to operate with maximum effectiveness.

5. The Sociology of Religion and Pastoral Care

1. Some sociologists of religion use different terminology to refer to alienating and de-alienating religion. They prefer to speak of reification instead of alienation and to contrast reified and de-reified religion.

Throughout our discussion, we use the former terms for ease of understanding.

2. See Catholic theologian Gregory Baum (1975) for a comprehensive examination of religion as alienation.

3. The loss of women's independent economic status after 400 A.D. with the fall of the Roman market economy and the rise of the fortified household economy resulted in the subordination of women in the medieval church.

6. The Institutional Context of Pastoral Care

1. See my article, "Healing Prayer and Pastoral Care," for an extended discussion of divine healing in hospital pastoral care (1984).

2. The recent publicized case of U. S. Air Force Chaplain Garland L. Robertson (Schmitt 1993; Sehested 1994) involves a military chaplain whose commitment to his religious faith and church took precedence over his military office. Lt. Col. Robertson, a decorated Vietnam pilot, undertook theological training, was ordained in the Southern Baptist church, earned a doctorate in ethics, and had served as a chaplain for nine years. Two weeks before the start of the Gulf War, he wrote a letter to the editor of a local newspaper in Texas near his base questioning the use of force against Iraq. In the letter, Robertson challenged Vice President Quayle's message to U. S. troops in Saudi Arabia that the American people were solidly behind a military offensive against Saddam Hussein. Soldiers needed to understand, Robertson said, that the American people were not united in support of the war. Base commanders took action against Robertson, leading ultimately to an Air Force board of inquiry decision to force him out of the service and to deny him his military pension. After exhausting the hearings process, Robertson appealed his case to the Secretary of the Air Force. At the time of writing (May 1994), he awaits the Secretary's decision on his status and pension. Robertson reports (personal conversation) that he visited the Pentagon in April 1994 and learned that a large number of letters had reached Air Force headquarters expressing support for his action.

3. For an investigation of the socialization of liberal Protestant seminary students that examines the dilemmas of professionalization, role conflict, and humanistic versus transcendent worldviews, see sociologist Sherryl Kleinman's participant-observation study (1984) of "Midwest Seminary."

4. Newbigin bases his position on Michael Polanyi, Alastair McIntyre, and Peter Berger. Polanyi and McIntyre are also important sources for the "postliberal" so-called "Yale School of Theology" (George Lindbeck, David Kelsey, Brevard Childs) described by Placher (1989). Newbigin's view that religious knowledge is public truth aligns him on this particular issue with

the "revisionist" theologians Schubert Ogden, David Tracy, and James Gustafson rather than the "postliberals." Robert Bellah (1989), while sympathetic to Lindbeck's general approach, opposes its parochialism and presses for world religious dialogue à la Newbigin.

7. Pastoral Care as Social Process

1. The chaplain has in mind "the upside-down kingdom" as described by such theologians as Donald Kraybill (1978).

Glossary

alienation   The process whereby human beings lose awareness of the fact their culture is a human construction.

alienating religion   Religious perspectives that obscure realization of the human construction of the social order.

cathectic orientations   Ideas about emotions and feelings. Term comes from the word *cathexis*, the investment of mental or emotional energy in a person, object, or idea.

cognitive dissonance   The mental strain caused by trying to hold on to two contrary ideas at the same time.

cognitive orientations   Ideas about the facts of reality answering the questions, What is? What is true and factual?

conflict tradition   Sociologists who view social life as a struggle for power. This perspective assigns major importance to people's economic, political, and prestige "interests."

cosmopolitans   Persons who are oriented to regional, national, and world events.

culture   A society's symbols and their meanings; the filter between stimulus and response that governs people's selective perceptions.

delegitimation of religious experience   Perceptions of spiritual reality are denied truth-value and are classified as "fiction" rather than "fact."

de-alienating religion   Religious beliefs that express an original theological vision. A transcendent perspective that judges the human social order.

differentiation   The sense of boundaries between the self and others.

elective affinity   The process whereby adherents of a religious belief-system choose to emphasize certain of its ideas that serve their economic and political interests; other persons with those same interests join the religious group.

ethos   The way of life of a people, especially its social rituals. The ethos reflects the cathectic and evaluative orientations of a society in contrast to the worldview, which is the cognitive orientation.

evaluative orientations   Moral and ethical ideas answering the questions, What is right? What is the good?

family systems therapy   A style of psychological counseling associated with Murray Bowen, Jay Haley, and others that stresses the family as a social system and the problems of the members as qualities of the group interactional process.

functions, social functions   The positive consequences of particular social customs and practices for the adaptation and integration of societies. Negative consequences are called "dysfunctions."

functionalism, functionalists   Sociologists who assess the effects of social norms and values for societal survival and optimum operation. They sometimes hold the idea that a society is a self-regulating system tending toward social homeostasis or equilibrium.

gender, gender stratification   Definitions of the situation regarding male and female identities; the power differences between male and female people.

generalized other   A mental construct of "society" that orients people's social identity.

hierophany   A dramatic religious experience perceived as a breaking in of transcendent reality.

homeless mind   The modern social psychological condition in which stable anchorages for one's identity are absent; do-it-yourself cognitive world.

latent functions   The consequences of social norms and customs that are not recognized by the performers. Sometimes called "unanticipated consequences."

locals Persons oriented to the geographically proximate community and its social dynamics.

manifest functions The intended consequences of human behavior.

mediating structures A level of groupings and associations, such as churches, town councils, labor union locals, and voluntary associations, between the individual's primary groups and the national society's megastructures.

modern society, modernity The society characterized by urbanization, industrialization, mass media of communication, and cultural pluralism.

modes of consciousness The multiple levels of reality of which people are aware.

organizational culture The distinctive values and norms of a particular organization such as a corporation, church, or association.

pastoral care A therapeutic modality distinguished by the dialogue of caregiver and careseeker that explores the possibility and implications of a religious definition of the latter's situation.

personal identity That part of the social self stressing one's differentiation from others.

phenomenology, phenomenological tradition The study of human consciousness open to the full complexity of the observed human subject, who is the "phenomenon."

plausibility structure The complex of social interactions that reinforce a worldview.

power The capacity of a society to define and achieve its collective goals. The capacity of one individual to enforce conformity from another against the latter's will.

reality-maintenance Social rituals that provide confirmation for a worldview.

reference group The persons whose values and esteem orient the attitudes and identity of an individual.

relative deprivation Assessment of one's situation in terms of what others have or do not have. Contrasts with absolute deprivation.

religion, religious definition of the situation   Beliefs, practices, and groupings oriented to transcendent or supernatural reality.

role   The set of expectations that others have for the occupant of a social position.

role-set   The position-occupants who typically influence the actions of the occupant of a focal position.

role conflict   Lack of consensus about a position-occupant's role among significant others.

routinization of charisma   The adaptation of a religious movement to "life in the world."

secularization   The reduction of the social influence of religion in a society; the delegitimation of religious experience.

social construction of reality   A "symbolic universe" created by human beings through externalization, objectification, and identification.

social identity   That part of the social self stressing one's identification with others.

social self   The combination of one's social identity and one's personal identity.

socialization   A structured social relationship for the purpose of enhancing learning, coping, and developing new attitudes and perspectives.

socializing the difficulty   Anton Boisen's term for expressing one's inner conflict to other people.

sociology of knowledge   The branch of sociology focused on the social basis for people's definitions of the situation.

sociology of religion   The study of the institutional sector of religion and its interface with other sectors.

status inconsistency   Unequal ranking of an individual's social positions.

stratification   Differentiation of a society's population in terms of economic resources, power, and social prestige.

structural differentiation   One multifunctional system divides into two or more systems, each with a specific function.

symbolic universe   The complex of symbols that mediate our contact with the universe.

Thomas theorem   The subjective perception of the situation is just as important in terms of consequences as the objective reality.

traditional society A society without urbanization, industrialization, mass media, and cultural pluralism.

transcendence Beliefs about God as Other, standing over and against the creation. Also beliefs about a spiritual realm that surrounds the material world.

worldview A person's basic orientation to reality. Cognitive orientation. Contrasts with ethos.

Bibliography

Alves, Rubem. 1977. "Personal Wholeness and Political Creativity: The Theology of Liberation and Pastoral Care," *Pastoral Psychology* 26: 124–36.

Augsburger, David W. 1986. *Pastoral Counseling across Cultures.* Philadelphia: Westminster Press.

Bain, Homer. A. 1986. "The Pastoral Counselor as Prophet," *Journal of Pastoral Care* 40: 322–29.

Baum, Gregory. 1975. *Religion and Alienation.* New York: Paulist Press.

Bell, Daniel. 1976. *The Cultural Contradictions of Capitalism.* New York: Basic Books.

———. 1977. "The Return of the Sacred? The Argument on the Future of Religion," *British Journal of Sociology* 28: 419–49.

Bellah, Robert N. 1957. *Tokugawa Religion: The Values of Pre-industrial Japan.* Glencoe, Ill.: Free Press.

———. 1970. *Beyond Belief: Essays on Religion in a Post-Traditional World.* New York: Harper & Row.

_____. 1975. *The Broken Covenant: American Civil Religion in Time of Trial.* New York: Seabury Press.

_____. 1989. "Christian Faithfulness in a Pluralist World." In Frederic B. Burnham, ed., *Postmodern Theology: Christian Faith in a Pluralist World,* 74–91. New York: Harper & Row.

Bellah, Robert N., Richard Madsen, William M. Sullivan, Ann Swidler, and Steven M. Tipton. 1985. *Habits of the Heart: Individualism and Commitment in American Life.* Berkeley: University of California Press.

———. 1991. *The Good Society.* New York: Alfred A. Knopf.

Bendix, Reinhard. 1960. *Max Weber: An Intellectual Portrait.* Garden City, N.Y.: Doubleday & Co.

Berelson, Bernard, and Gary A. Steiner. 1964. *Human Behavior: An Inventory of Scientific Findings.* New York: Harcourt, Brace & World.

Berger, Peter L. 1963. *Invitation to Sociology: A Humanistic Perspective.* Garden City, N.Y.: Doubleday & Co.

————. 1967. *The Sacred Canopy: Elements of a Sociological Theory of Religion*. Garden City, N.Y.: Doubleday & Co.

————. 1969. *A Rumor of Angels: Modern Society and the Rediscovery of the Supernatural*. Garden City, N.Y.: Doubleday & Co.

————. 1974. "Some Second Thoughts on Substantive versus Functional Definitions of Religion," *Journal for the Scientific Study of Religion* 13: 125–33.

————. 1979. *The Heretical Imperative: Contemporary Possibilities of Religious Affirmation*. Garden City, N.Y.: Doubleday & Co., Anchor Books.

————. 1992. *A Far Glory: The Quest for Faith in an Age of Credulity*. New York: Free Press.

Berger, Peter L., Brigitte Berger, and Hansfried Kellner. 1973. *The Homeless Mind: Modernization and Consciousness*. New York: Random House.

Berger, Peter L., and Thomas Luckmann. 1966. *The Social Construction of Reality: A Treatise in the Sociology of Knowledge*. Garden City, N.Y.: Doubleday & Co.

Berger, Peter L., and Richard J. Neuhaus. 1977. *To Empower People: The Role of Mediating Structures in Public Policy*. Washington, D.C.: American Enterprise Institute for Public Policy Research.

Bernard, Jessie. 1972. *The Future of Marriage*. New York: World Publishing Co.

Blau, Peter M. 1963. *The Dynamics of Bureaucracy*. Chicago: University of Chicago Press.

Blumer, Herbert. 1969. *Symbolic Interactionism: Perspective and Method*. Englewood Cliffs, N.J.: Prentice-Hall.

Bocock, Robert. 1976. *Freud and Modern Society: An Outline and Analysis of Freud's Sociology*. Sunbury-on-Thames, Middlesex: Thomas Nelson.

Boisen, Anton T. 1928. "The Sense of Isolation in Mental Disorders: Its Religious Significance," *American Journal of Sociology* 33: 555–67.

————. 1955. *Religion in Crisis and Custom: A Sociological and Psychological Study*. New York: Harper & Brothers.

————. 1961. *Out of the Depths*. New York: Harper & Brothers.

Boss, Pauline, and Barrie Thorne. 1989. "Family Sociology and Family Therapy: A Feminist Linkage." In Monica McGoldrick, Carol M. Anderson, and Froma Walsh, *Women in Families: A Framework for Family Therapy*. New York: W. W. Norton & Co.

Bredemeier, Harry C., and Richard M. Stephenson. 1962. *The Analysis of Social Systems*. New York: Holt, Rinehart and Winston.

Browning, Don S. 1976. *The Moral Context of Pastoral Care*. Philadelphia: Westminster Press.

————. 1983. *Religious Ethics and Pastoral Care*. Philadelphia: Fortress Press.

————. 1987. *Religious Thought and the Modern Psychologies*. Philadelphia: Fortress Press.

_____. 1992. *A Fundamental Practical Theology: Descriptive and Strategic Proposals*. Minneapolis: Fortress Press.

Burchard, Waldo W. 1954. "Role Conflicts of Military Chaplains," *American Sociological Review* 19: 528–35.

Buxton, William. 1985. *Talcott Parsons and the Capitalist Nation-State: Political Sociology as a Strategic Vocation*. Toronto: University of Toronto Press.

Campbell, Alastair V. 1985. *Professionalism and Pastoral Care*. Philadelphia: Fortress Press.

Capps, Donald. 1984. *Pastoral Care and Hermeneutics*. Philadelphia: Fortress Press.

Carey, Raymond G. 1985. "Change in Perceived Need, Value and Role of Hospital Chaplains." In Lawrence E. Holst, ed., *Hospital Ministry*, 28–41. New York: Crossroad.

Carroll, Jackson W., Carl S. Dudley, and William McKinney, eds. 1986. *Handbook of Congregational Studies*. Nashville: Abingdon Press.

Chopp, Rebecca S. 1987. "Practical Theology and Liberation." In Lewis S. Mudge and James N. Poling, eds., *Formation and Reflection: The Promise of Practical Theology*, 120–38. Philadelphia: Fortress Press.

Chopp, Rebecca S., and Duane F. Parker. 1990. *Liberation Theology and Pastoral Theology*. Decatur, Ga.: Journal of Pastoral Care Publications.

Clark, Glenn. 1932. *The Lord's Prayer*. St. Paul: Macalester Park Publishing Co.

Clinebell, Charlotte Holt. 1976. *Counseling for Liberation*. Philadelphia: Fortress Press.

Clinebell, Howard. 1981. *Contemporary Growth Therapies: Resources for Actualizing Human Wholeness*. Nashville: Abingdon Press.

Collins, Randall. 1975. *Conflict Sociology: Toward an Explanatory Science*. New York: Academic Press.

_____. 1979. *The Credential Society: An Historical Sociology of Education and Stratification*. New York: Academic Press.

_____. 1985. *Three Sociological Traditions*. New York: Oxford University Press.

Cook, Gary A. 1993. *George Herbert Mead: The Making of a Social Pragmatist*. Urbana: University of Illinois Press.

Coser, Lewis A. 1971. *Masters of Sociological Thought: Ideas in Historical and Social Context*. New York: Harcourt Brace Jovanovich.

Coser, Ruth Laub. 1991. *In Defense of Modernity: Role Complexity and Individual Autonomy*. Stanford, Calif.: Stanford University Press.

Davis, Kingsley, and Wilbert E. Moore. 1945. "Some Principles of Stratification," *American Sociological Review* 10: 242–49.

Duffy, Regis A., O.F.M. 1983. *A Roman Catholic Theology of Pastoral Care*. Philadelphia: Fortress Press.

Durkheim, Émile. 1915. *The Elementary Forms of the Religious Life*. Trans. Joseph W. Swain. London: George Allen & Unwin.

_____. 1938. *The Rules of the Sociological Method*. Trans. Sarah A. Solovay and John H. Mueller. George E. G. Catlin, ed. Chicago: University of Chicago Press.

_____. 1951. *Suicide: A Study in Sociology*. Trans. George Simpson. New York: Free Press.

Evans-Pritchard, E. E. 1940. *The Nuer*. Oxford: Clarendon Press.

Farley, Edward. 1975. *Ecclesial Man: A Social Phenomenology of Faith and Reality*. Philadelphia: Fortress Press.

_____. 1977. "Phenomenology and Pastoral Care," *Pastoral Psychology* 26: 95–112.

Fitzgerald, C. George. 1993. *The Supervision of Congregational Ministries: The Reflective Practice of Ministry*. Decatur, Ga.: Journal of Pastoral Care Publications.

Fowler, James W. 1987. *Faith Development and Pastoral Care*. Philadelphia: Fortress Press.

Fowler, Gene T., Jr. 1990. "Caring for Society." In Leroy Aden and J. Harold Ellens, eds., *Turning Points in Pastoral Care: The Legacy of Anton Boisen and Seward Hiltner*, 205–23. Grand Rapids: Baker Book House.

Fox, Renée C. 1989. *The Sociology of Medicine*. Englewood Cliffs, N.J.: Prentice-Hall.

Fox-Genovese, Elizabeth. 1991. *Feminism Without Illusions: A Critique of Individualism*. Chapel Hill: University of North Carolina Press.

Friedman, Edwin H. 1985. *Generation to Generation: Family Process in Church and Synagogue*. New York: Guilford Press.

Furniss, George M. 1984. "Healing Prayer and Pastoral Care," *Journal of Pastoral Care* 38: 107–19.

_____. 1992. "The Forest and the Trees: The Value of Sociology for Pastoral Care," *Journal of Pastoral Care* 46: 349–60.

Garfinkel, Harold. 1967. *Studies in Ethnomethodology*. Englewood Cliffs, N.J.: Prentice-Hall.

Garrett, William R. 1979. "Reference Groups and Role Strains Related to Spiritual Well-Being," *Sociological Analysis* 40: 43–58.

Geertz, Clifford. 1966. "Religion as a Cultural System." In Michael Banton, ed., *Anthropological Approaches to the Study of Religion*, 1–46. London: Tavistock Publications.

Gerkin, Charles V. 1984. *The Living Human Document: Re-Visioning Pastoral Counseling in a Hermeneutical Mode*. Nashville: Abingdon Press.

_____. 1986. *Widening the Horizons: Pastoral Responses to a Fragmented Society*. Philadelphia: Westminster Press.

Giddens, Anthony. 1984. *The Constitution of Society: Outline of the Theory of Structuration*. Berkeley: University of California Press.

Glaz, Maxine, and Jeanne Stevenson Moessner, eds. 1991. *Women in Travail and Transition: A New Pastoral Care*. Minneapolis: Fortress Press.

Goffman, Erving. 1959. *The Presentation of Self in Everyday Life*. Garden City, N.Y.: Doubleday & Co.

_____. 1963. *Stigma: Notes on the Management of Spoiled Identity*. Englewood Cliffs, N.J.: Prentice-Hall.

_____. 1987. "The Arrangement between the Sexes," *Theory and Society* 4 (1977): 301–31. Reprinted in Mary Jo Deegan and Michael R. Hill, eds. *Women and Symbolic Interaction*. Boston: Allen & Unwin.

Graham, Larry Kent. 1992. *Care of Persons, Care of Worlds: A Psychosystems Approach to Pastoral Care and Counseling*. Nashville: Abingdon Press.

Gross, Neal, Ward S. Mason, and Alexander W. McEachern. 1958. *Explorations in Role Analysis: Studies of the School Superintendency Role*. New York: John Wiley.

Habermas, Jürgen. 1975. *Legitimation Crisis*. Trans. Thomas McCarthy. Boston: Beacon Press.

Hall, Charles E. 1992. *Head and Heart: The Story of the Clinical Pastoral Education Movement*. Decatur, Ga.: Journal of Pastoral Care Publications.

Hargrove, Barbara, ed. 1984. *Religion and the Sociology of Knowledge: Modernization and Pluralism in Christian Thought and Structure*. (Studies in Religion and Society Series, No. 8) New York: Edwin Mellen Press.

Haroutunian, Joseph. 1965. *God with Us: A Theology of Transpersonal Life*. Philadelphia: Westminster Press.

Hauerwas, Stanley. 1981. *A Community of Character: Toward a Constructive Christian Social Ethic*. Notre Dame, Ind.: University of Notre Dame Press.

Haugk, Kenneth C. 1984. *Christian Caregiving: A Way of Life*. Minneapolis: Augsburg.

Heilman, Samuel C. 1976. *Synagogue Life: A Study in Symbolic Interaction*. Chicago: University of Chicago Press.

Hewitt, John P. 1989. *Dilemmas of the American Self*. Philadelphia: Temple University Press.

Holst, Lawrence E. 1985. "The Hospital Chaplain: Between Worlds." in L. E. Holst, ed., *Hospital Ministry: The Role of the Chaplain Today*, 12–27. New York: Crossroad.

Holmes, Urban T. 1982. *Spirituality for Ministry*. San Francisco: Harper & Row.

Hopewell, James F. 1987. *Congregation: Stories and Structures*. Philadelphia: Fortress Press.

Hunter, James D., and Stephen C. Ainlay, eds. 1986. *Making Sense of Modern Times: Peter L. Berger and the Vision of Interpretive Sociology*. London: Routledge & Kegan Paul.

Hunter, Rodney J. 1979. "Moltmann's Theology of the Cross and the Dilemma of Contemporary Pastoral Care." In Theodore Runyon, ed., *Hope for the Church: Moltmann in Dialogue with Practical Theology*, 75–92. Nashville: Abingdon Press.

Jackson, Gordon E. 1981. *Pastoral Care and Process Theology.* Washington, D.C.: University Press of America.

Johnson, Benton. 1963. "On Church and Sect," *American Sociological Review* 28: 539–49.

Johnson, Terence J. 1972. *Professions and Power.* London: Macmillan Publishers.

Jonakeit, Randolph N. 1973. *The Abuses of the Military Chaplaincy.* ACLU Reports: American Civil Liberties Union, May 1973.

Kelley, Dean M. 1972. *Why Conservative Churches Are Growing.* New York: Harper & Row.

Kelsey, Morton T. 1972. *Encounter with God: A Theology of Christian Experience.* Minneapolis: Bethany Fellowship Press.

_____. 1982. *Prophetic Ministry: The Psychology and Spirituality of Pastoral Care.* New York: Crossroad.

Kinast, Robert L. 1980. "The Pastoral Care of Society as Liberation," *Journal of Pastoral Care* 34: 125–30.

Kleinman, Sherryl. 1984. *Equals before God: Seminarians as Humanistic Professionals.* Chicago: University of Chicago Press.

Kornhauser, William. 1959. *The Politics of Mass Society.* Glencoe, Ill.: Free Press.

Kraybill, Donald B. 1978. *The Upside-Down Kingdom.* Scottdale, Pa.: Herald Press.

LaCugna, Catherine M. 1992. *God for Us: The Trinity and Christian Life.* San Francisco: HarperCollins.

Lake, Frank. 1987. *Clinical Theology: A Theological and Psychological Basis to Clinical Pastoral Care.* Abridged by Martin H. Yeomans. New York: Crossroad. [Unabridged edition published in Britain, 1966]

Lambourne, R. A. 1963. *Community, Church and Healing.* London: Darton, Longman & Todd.

Larson, Magali Sarfatti. 1977. *The Rise of Professionalism: A Sociological Analysis.* Berkeley: University of California Press.

Lasch, Christopher. 1978. *The Culture of Narcissism: American Life in an Age of Diminishing Expectations.* New York: W. W. Norton & Co.

Leinberger, Paul, and Bruce Tucker. 1991. *The New Individualists: The Generation after the Organization Man.* San Francisco: HarperCollins.

Lenski, Gerhard E. 1966. *Power and Privilege: A Theory of Social Stratification.* New York: McGraw-Hill.

Lenski, Gerhard E., and Jean Lenski. 1974. *Human Societies: An Introduction to Macrosociology,* 2d ed. New York: McGraw-Hill.

LIFO Training. 1978. Beverly Hills, Calif.: Stuart Adkins, Inc.

Lippmann, Walter. 1922. *Public Opinion.* New York: Harcourt, Brace & Co.

Luhmann, Niklas. 1982. *The Differentiation of Society.* New York: Columbia University Press.

Lukes, Steven. 1973. *Émile Durkheim, His Life and Work: A Historical and Critical Study*. Harmondsworth, England: Penguin.

Lynch, James J. 1977. *The Broken Heart: The Medical Consequences of Loneliness*. New York: Basic Books.

Malinowski, Bronislaw. 1954. *Magic, Science and Religion, and Other Essays*. Garden City, N.Y.: Doubleday.

Mannheim, Karl. 1936. *Ideology and Utopia: An Introduction to the Sociology of Knowledge*. Trans. Louis Wirth and Edward Shils. New York: Harcourt, Brace.

Martin, David, John O. Mills, and W.S.F. Pickering. 1980. *Sociology and Theology: Alliance and Conflict*. New York: St. Martin's Press.

Mead, George Herbert. 1962. *Mind, Self, and Society: From the Standpoint of a Social Behaviorist*. Ed. Charles W. Morris. Chicago: University of Chicago Press.

Merton, Robert K. 1957. *Social Theory and Social Structure*. Rev. ed. Glencoe, Ill.: Free Press.

Mills, C. Wright. 1967. *The Sociological Imagination*. New York: Oxford University Press.

Moessner, Jeanne Stevenson, and Maxine Glaz. 1991. "Introduction: I Heard a Cry." In M. Glaz and J. S. Moessner, eds., *Women in Travail and Transition: A New Pastoral Care*. Minneapolis: Fortress Press.

Mudge, Lewis S., and James N. Poling. 1987. "Introduction." In L. S. Mudge and J. N. Poling, eds., *Formation and Reflection: The Promise of Practical Theology*, xiii–xxxvi. Philadelphia: Fortress Press.

Newbigin, Lesslie. 1989. *The Gospel in a Pluralist Society*. Grand Rapids: Wm. B. Eerdmans.

Niebuhr, H. Richard. 1929. *The Social Sources of Denominationalism*. New York: Henry Holt.

———. 1963. *The Responsible Self: An Essay in Christian Moral Philosophy*. New York: Harper & Row.

Nouwen, Henri J. M. 1972. *The Wounded Healer: Ministry in Contemporary Society*. Garden City, N.Y.: Doubleday & Co.

Oates, Wayne E. 1973. *The Psychology of Religion*. Waco, Tex.: Word Books.

Palmer, Stuart. 1981. *Role Stress: How to Handle Everyday Tension*. Englewood Cliffs, N.J.: Prentice-Hall.

Parsons, Talcott. 1937. *The Structure of Social Action*. Glencoe, Ill.: Free Press.

———. 1951. *The Social System*. Glencoe, Ill.: Free Press.

———. 1964. *Social Structure and Personality*. New York: Free Press of Glencoe.

———. 1969. *Politics and Social Structure*. New York: Free Press.

———. 1977. *The Evolution of Societies*. Ed. Jackson Toby. Englewood Cliffs, N.J.: Prentice-Hall.

Parsons, Talcott, and Robert F. Bales. 1955. *Family, Socialization, and Interaction Process*. Glencoe, Ill.: Free Press.

Pattison, E. Mansell. 1972. "Systems Pastoral Care," *Journal of Pastoral Care* 26: 2–14.

_____. 1977. *Pastor and Parish: A Systems Approach.* Philadelphia: Fortress Press.

Pattison, Stephen. 1988. *A Critique of Pastoral Care.* London: SCM Press.

Payne, Leanne. 1989. *The Healing Presence.* Wheaton, Ill.: Crossway.

Perkins, Richard B. 1987. *Looking Both Ways: Exploring the Interface between Christianity and Sociology.* Grand Rapids: Baker Book House.

Peters, Ted. 1993. *God as Trinity: Relationality and Temporality in Divine Life.* Louisville, Ky.: Westminster/John Knox Press.

Peters, Thomas J., and Robert H. Waterman, Jr. 1982. *In Search of Excellence: Lessons from America's Best-Run Companies.* New York: Harper & Row.

Phillips, J. B. 1953. *Your God Is Too Small.* New York: Macmillan Publishing Co.

Placher, William C. 1989. *Unapologetic Theology: A Christian Voice in a Pluralistic Conversation.* Louisville, Ky.: Westminster/John Knox Press.

Pruyser, Paul W. 1967. "Anton T. Boisen and the Psychology of Religion," *Journal of Pastoral Care* 21: 209–19.

_____. 1976. *The Minister as Diagnostician: Personal Problems in Pastoral Perspective.* Philadelphia: Westminster Press.

Rieff, Philip. 1966. *The Triumph of the Therapeutic.* New York: Harper & Row.

_____. 1990. *The Feeling Intellect.* Chicago: University of Chicago Press.

Riesman, David, with Nathan Glazer and Reuel Denney. 1950. *The Lonely Crowd: A Study of the Changing American Character.* New Haven: Yale University Press.

Roof, Wade Clark. 1978. *Community and Commitment: Religious Plausibility in a Liberal Protestant Church.* New York: Elsevier.

Sanford, Agnes. 1947. *The Healing Light.* St. Paul, Minn.: Macalester Park Publishing Co.

_____. 1972. *Sealed Orders.* Plainfield, N.J.: Logos International.

Sarason, Seymour. 1971. *The Culture of the School and the Problem of Change.* Rockleigh, N.J.: Allyn & Bacon.

Schleiermacher, Friedrich. 1968. *On Religion: Speeches to Its Cultured Despisers.* Orig. pub. 1799. Trans. John Oman. New York: Harper & Row.

Schmidt, Alvin J. 1978. "The Great Omission in Ministerial Education: Sociological Awareness." In Gaylord B. Noyce, ed., *Education for Ministry: Theology, Preparedness, Praxis.* Report of the 15th Biennial Meeting of the Association for Professional Education for Ministry, Trinity College, Toronto, Ontario. June 17–19, 1978: 94–100.

Schmitt, Eric. 1993. "Military Chaplain Fights a Battle over Loyalties," *New York Times.* Dec. 21, 1993, A8.

Schreiter, Robert J. 1985. *Constructing Local Theologies.* Maryknoll, N.Y.: Orbis Books.

Schutz, Alfred. 1962. "On Multiple Realities." In his *Collected Papers* I: 207–59. The Hague: Martinus Nijhoff.

Sehested, Ken. l994. "Loyalty Test: The Case of Chaplain Robertson," *The Christian Century* 111: 212–14.

Seifert, Harvey, and Howard Clinebell. 1974. *Personal Growth and Social Change*. Philadelphia: Westminster Press.

Shibutani, Tamotsu. 1961. *Society and Personality: An Interactionist Approach to Social Psychology*. Englewood Cliffs, N.J.: Prentice-Hall.

Slater, Philip. 1970. *The Pursuit of Loneliness: American Culture at the Breaking Point*. Boston: Beacon Press.

Smail, Thomas A. 1980. *The Forgotten Father*. Grand Rapids: Wm. B. Eerdmans.

Smith, Archie, Jr. 1982. *The Relational Self: Ethics and Therapy from a Black Church Perspective*. Nashville: Abingdon Press.

Simonton, O. Carl, Stephanie Matthews-Simonton, and James Creighton. 1978. *Getting Well Again: A Step-by-Step, Self-help Guide to Overcoming Cancer for Patients and Their Families*. Los Angeles: J. P. Tarcher.

Stark, Rodney, and William S. Bainbridge. 1985. *The Future of Religion: Secularization, Revival, and Cult Formation*. Berkeley: University of California Press.

———. 1987. *A Theory of Religion*. New York: Peter Lang.

Stark, Rodney, and Charles Y. Glock. 1968. *American Piety: The Nature of Religious Commitment*. Berkeley: University of California Press, 1968.

Strunk, Orlo, Jr. 1965. *Mature Religion: A Psychological Study*. Nashville: Abingdon Press.

Swatos, William H., Jr. 1987. "Clinical Pastoral Sociology." In W. H. Swatos, ed., *Religious Sociology: Interfaces and Boundaries*, 153–64. New York: Greenwood Press.

Thayer, Nelson S. T. 1985. *Spirituality and Pastoral Care*. Philadelphia: Fortress Press.

Thomas, William I. 1923. *The Unadjusted Girl*. Boston: Little, Brown & Co.

Thomas, William I., and Dorothy Swaine Thomas. 1928. *The Child in America*. New York: Alfred A. Knopf.

Thornton, Edward E. 1970. *Professional Education for Ministry: A History of Clinical Pastoral Education*. Nashville: Abingdon Press.

Thurow, Lester C. 1985. *The Zero-Sum Solution: Building a World-Class American Economy*. New York: Simon & Schuster.

Tinlin, Paul B., and Edith L. Blumhofer. 1991. "Decade of Decline or Harvest? Dilemmas of the Assemblies of God," *The Christian Century* 108: 684–87.

Tocqueville, Alexis de. 1961. *Democracy in America*. Orig. pub. 1835. Trans. Henry Reeve. New York: Schocken Books.

Tumin, Melvin M. 1953. "Some Principles of Stratification: A Critical Analysis," *American Sociological Review* 18: 387–94.

Unterberger, Gail. 1990. "Through the Lens of Feminine Psychology and Feminine Theology: A Theoretical Model for Pastoral Counseling." Ph.D. dissertation, School of Theology at Claremont.

Van Wagner, Charles A. II. 1992. *The AAPC: A History of the American Association of Pastoral Counselors, 1963–1991*. Fairfax, N.J.: American Association of Pastoral Counselors.

Vickers, Robert C. 1984. "The Military Chaplaincy: A Study in Role Conflict." Ed.D. dissertation, Vanderbilt University.

Weber, Max. 1947a. "Science as a Vocation." In *From Max Weber: Essays in Sociology*, 129–56. Translated, edited, with an introduction by Hans H. Gerth and C. Wright Mills. New York: Oxford University Press.

_____. 1947b. *The Theory of Economic and Social Organization*. Trans. A. M. Henderson and Talcott Parsons. Glencoe, Ill.: Free Press.

_____. 1958. *The Protestant Ethic and the Spirit of Capitalism*. Trans. Talcott Parsons. New York: Charles Scribner's Sons. [Original German edition, 1905]

_____. 1968. *Economy and Society: An Outline of Interpretive Sociology*. Ed. Guenther Roth and Claus Wittich. New York: Bedminster Press.

Westerhoff, John H. III, and Gwen Kennedy Neville. 1974. *Generation to Generation: Conversations on Religious Education and Culture*. Philadelphia: United Church Press.

Whitehead, James D., and Evelyn Eaton Whitehead. 1980. *Method in Ministry: Theological Reflection and Christian Ministry*. San Francisco: HarperCollins.

Whyte, William Foote. 1943. *Street Corner Society: The Social Structure of an Italian Slum*. Chicago: University of Chicago Press.

Williams, Robert. 1978. *Schleiermacher the Theologian: The Construction of the Doctrine of God*. Philadelphia: Fortress Press.

Wilson, Bryan. 1982. *Religion in Sociological Perspective*. New York: Oxford University Press.

Wilson, William J. 1987. *The Truly Disadvantaged: The Inner City, the Underclass, and Public Policy*. Chicago: University of Chicago Press.

Winter, J. Alan. 1977. *Continuities in the Sociology of Religion: Creed, Congregation, and Community*. New York: Harper & Row.

Witz, Anne. 1992. *Professions and Patriarchy*. London: Routledge & Kegan Paul.

Wolff, Pierre. 1979. *May I Hate God?* New York: Paulist Press.

Index